AT

The Political Branding of Oliver North

DR. GARY AMOS

Integrity Press
Virginia Beach, Virginia

Published September 1994. First Addition, pocket paperback.
First Printing, September 1994.

Printed in the United States of America.
ISBN 0-9643427-0-7

Unless otherwise noted, all Scripture quotations are from the King James Version of the Bible.

Published by:
Integrity Press
P.O. Box 9172
Virginia Beach, VA 23450-9172
(800) 575-6648, (804) 485-9307

Printed by:
Faith Printing
4210 Locust Hill Rd.
Taylors, SC 29687-8911

Cover Design by:
Graphicom
P.O. Box 10720
Ft. Worth, Texas 76114-0720
(817) 625-5500

THIS BOOK IS DEDICATED TO

unsung patriot heroes, veterans of America's wars, from my hometown of Boones Mill, Virginia (population 256). Some of these are:

- RAYMOND AMOS, my dad, who won four bronze stars and the silver star for meritorious service in WWII; a veteran of the D-Day invasion and of all five major campaigns in the European theater.
- CANEY CLEMONS, 82d Airborne, killed in action taking a bridge in Belgium, WWII.
- BUFORD CLEMONS, Caney's brother, disabled for life, suffering massive internal injuries from a blast concussion, fighting the Japanese in the Philippines, WWII.
- HAROLD MOORE, a private pilot who volunteered for the Canadian RAF to fight Hitler before the U.S. officially entered the war. Shot down and killed.
- NORMAN SINK and BOB BOITNOTT, both killed in action in WWII.
- BUDDY BUSSEY, TOUNES DUNAHOO [POW], and HERMAN WEBSTER, WWII.
- MICHAEL CANNADAY, PFC U.S. Army, who died on New Years Day 1967, Viet Nam.

To these and to the numerous other veterans from Boones Mill, who served in WWI, WWII, Korea, and Viet Nam – Thank you for freedom!

"No Bill of Attainder or ex post facto Law shall be passed." [U.S. Constitution, Article 1, Section 9, Clause 3.]

Attaint: To condemn by a sentence of attainder. To impart stigma to; to disgrace. To accuse or prove guilty. [American Heritage Dictionary]

Attainder: The loss of . . . civil rights. Dishonor."

Bill of Attainder: A . . . legislative act pronouncing a person guilty of a crime, usually treason, without trial. [American Heritage Dictionary.]

"Legislative acts, no matter what their form, that apply either to named individuals or to easily ascertainable members of a group in such a way as to inflict punishment on them without judicial trial are bills of attainder prohibited by the Constitution."

U.S. v Lovett, 328 U.S. 303, 315, 90 L.Ed. 1252.
United States Supreme Court (June 3, 1946).

"When our Constitution and Bill of Rights were written, our ancestors had ample reason to know that legislative trials and punishments were too dangerous to liberty to exist in the nation of free men they envisioned. And so they proscribed bills of attainder."

U.S. v Lovett, 328 U.S. 318.

"The political needs of the majority, or Congress, or the President never, never, never should trump an individual's explicit constitutional protections."

U.S. v North, 920 F.2d 940, 946 (Nov. 30, 1990).
United States Court of Appeals

TABLE OF CONTENTS

INTRODUCTION

This book is about a political outrage. It is about the machinery of government run amok. It is about a seven year vendetta by the politically powerful to pursue, crush, and ruin a scapegoat, an underdog – a citizen.

But that is not all. It is about the trashing of the United States Constitution by politicians, and their concerted attempt to deceive ordinary Americans. It is about our own gullibility as citizens and our ignorance of the Constitution.

It is about a defeat suffered by you, and me, and our country. And also it is about how you and I, through our own ignorance and silence, have been accomplices to the most serious attack on the Constitution in our lifetimes.

Don't think that this book was written to help win an election. The stakes are much higher than that. To think that this book was written to firm up one man's political support misses the point. Besides, his support is already stronger than concrete.

The people who need this book the most are the people who already distrust Oliver North because of the televised hearings in the summer of 1987. This book is written especially for his critics and opponents.

If you dislike him, distrust him, disdain him, or even hate him, then this book is for you.

If you believe that Oliver North lied to Congress, or that he violated the Constitution and laws of the United States, then this book is for you.

If you are one who believes that he committed treason, was a traitor to his country, or broke his soldier's oath to defend the U.S. Constitution against all enemies foreign and domestic, you need this book.

Above all, if you are one of those who still calls him a convicted felon, and still insists that he was "let off on a technicality," you need the information in this book. Brace yourself. You are in for a real shock.

Now for some ground rules so you will know what to expect. Like you, I'm extremely busy. I am a lawyer, businessman, husband, and father. I have four weeks to write this book, in my "spare" time. Nobody asked me to write it. I'm not a hired gun. The book is not funded, subsidized, or supported in any way by the North campaign or anyone else. I'm doing it on my own time, on my own money, and all by myself.

My goals are modest, namely, to be precise, concise, simple, and clear. This is plain vanilla. At times the writing may seem rough, rude, needlessly repetitive, or overly blunt. But if you can look past the flaws and the purple prose, you will be surprised at the eye opening information inside. To the disappointed critic wishing for more interesting stories, anecdotes, figures of speech, and endearing techniques from a writer's workshop, call me. Who knows? With your help, and another four weeks, maybe the revised and expanded edition could win a Pulitzer.

ONE

Prelude to Scandal

My interest in Oliver North actually began before I ever heard his name or ever heard of Iran/Contra. It was Fall 1986. I had been invited to the White House for a policy briefing in the Old Executive Office Building. In those days I was a university professor teaching law and government. I was working on a book about the Declaration of Independence, and was doing a great deal of research into the writings of the Founding Fathers and how our country was founded.

During the briefing, one speaker – an assistant to a cabinet secretary – said glowingly, "We are proud to say that we have the best 'cabinet' form of government since the administration of John Quincy Adams."

"Uh oh," I muttered to myself as I began staring at the floor. "Nobody's minding the store." I felt a distinctly cold sense of foreboding, realizing that it was only a matter of time until the Reagan administration was rocked with a major scandal from within. When the Captain is not at the helm, major mistakes cannot be avoided.

This revelation could not have come at a worse time. The White House was already under siege from a hostile Congress dominated by the opposition party. The President had to devote far too much time taking his case to the public by means of personal appearances, local media, and end-runs around the Washington press corps. Age and gunshot wounds compounded the problem. In many ways, the White House was already on the defensive. Soon it would be on the ropes.

The four hour drive home to Virginia Beach caused me to arrive sometime after midnight. I tried to get ready for bed without waking my wife. But if I'm anything, it's clumsy. Stirring from a deep sleep, she asked groggily "how was your meeting?"

"You're not going to believe this," I told her, "there's nobody running the show." "You're kidding," she said. "Nope," I replied. "It's only a matter of time until a major scandal erupts."

At class, the students eagerly awaited being briefed on my trip. I repeated what the assistant secretary had said and gave my interpretation. I then told them to expect a major scandal any day, probably within a month. I hate being right.

It had already begun. On October 5, 1986, Eugene Hasenfus was shot down over Central America carrying supplies to the Contras in Nicaragua. Weeks later, on November 3, a Lebanese newspaper reported a secret arms sale to Iran from the U.S. On November 25, Attorney General Ed Meese announced that some of the proceeds of the sale had been diverted to help the Contras in Nicaragua. The torch was lit.

The President had one of two choices. He could take the high road and defend the constitutional powers of the presidency, following the example of Abraham Lincoln. This meant that he would face off with Congress on the point of the President's constitutional authority to control foreign affairs.

Instead the President took the low road, wanting to avoid such a face off. He denied any knowledge of what was going on, and left his lieutenants hanging out to dry. Age and injury meant there would not be one more for the Gipper. Like Gen. Winfield Scott, he had become old Fuss and Feathers.

His political opponents smelled blood. Here was their chance to avenge their losses in his first term and the embarrassing landslide re-election. They all knew, or at least suspected, that the policy was his. An operation of this size required so many people to be involved that links to the President would surely be found during an investigation.

With the right evidence, Congress could try to impeach him. At the very least they could investigate his administration to the point of paralyzing it. The major media would have a field day, obviously. For the president's political opposition, this was a chance to try to "Nixonize" another Republican president, and keep the White House safe for the democrats for the next four year term.

The FBI began to investigate on November 26, 1986. The President appointed the Tower Commission on December 1. And the Attorney General requested the appointment of an Independent Counsel on December 4. Lawrence Walsh was appointed to that position on December 19. He filed his final report on August 4, 1993.

By the end of December 1986, a number of senior government officials had given testimony during the investigation. It was clear from the press reports that some were running for the tall grass. Every finger was pointing to Oliver North. By January 1987, it was clear that North had been selected as the principal scapegoat, along with his superior, John Poindexter.

Then the talk turned to criminal indictments and sending people to jail. When North and Poindexter asserted their constitutional right not to testify against themselves, a number of congressmen loudly wailed that this proved their criminal guilt. The political lynch mob was already forming, being led by members of Congress. At the same time a compliant news media was already convicting North in newspapers all across the country.

Watching these events from afar, I was amazed at all the wasted opportunities by the White House to make its constitutional case to the public. Why were they running? There was no violation of the Constitution or of valid laws here! Why had they not gone on the offensive? Why were they not standing up for North and Poindexter rather than abandoning them on the beaches?

My letter in early February 1987 to an acquaintance with ties to the Vice President's office soon provided me with the answer. I learned that the wagons had been circled around the President and the Vice President to shield them from responsibility. My letter, advising a constitutional legal argument in defense of the President and of North, fell on deaf ears. The White House was not interested in defending North. It had chosen to disassociate itself from him. There would be no cowboy Reagan in this western. North was on his own, a truly perplexing response.

The Constitution, through the separation of powers, commits foreign policy primarily to the Executive Branch. The President is the one who formulates and carries out foreign policy. Since 1803 and the Marbury v. Madison Supreme Court case, it has been clear and settled that one branch of government cannot usurp the authority vested by the Constitution in another branch. Congress has no authority to restrict the foreign policy powers vested in the president by the Constitution.

For several years the majority party in Congress had tried to remove the president's ability to pursue his own foreign policy regarding Nicaragua and Central America. Reagan wanted to apply the Monroe doctrine and the Truman doctrine. This meant that he would use his powers as president to oppose the spread of communism in the western hemisphere. But the democrat majority fought him at every turn, and were aided by a continuous stream of misleading reports from the major media.

In the Fall of 1986, a steady avalanche of misinformation and inaccurate reporting had convinced large numbers of Americans that the Contras were "Somocistas" and "terrorists." Although it was untrue, a fact which is now widely known, the White House failed at the time to make its case to the public. The president failed to overcome the widely held impression that the Contras were the opposite of innocent victims and freedom fighters, and failed to convince the public of the strategic threat from long range bombers, missiles, and other weapons which were slated to be placed on Nicaraguan soil by the Sandinista communists.

In the face of a hostile press, a hostile Congress, and a divided public, the White House had a tough decision to make. Should it join the battle against the hostile Congress, wasting time and resources, or should the Executive Branch keep its primary focus on containing (and exhausting) communism and trying to make a dangerous world safer?

The choice was obvious. This was not the time for the United States to occupy itself with an internal struggle of constitutional proportions between the executive branch and the legislative branch. The President had to be free to focus almost all of his energies on being the leader of the free world.

TWO

Ollie in Wonderland

Lewis Carroll's *Through the Looking Glass* tells the story of Alice in Wonderland. In the story, Alice enters a world of mirror images where everything is reversed. This is what happened to Oliver North beginning in November 1986. He entered the mirror image world of power politics.

When the arms sales to Iran and the diversion of funds to the Contras came to light, Oliver North was immediately and incessantly accused of breaking the law and of violating the U.S. Constitution. These charges began in earnest when the Senate created its Select Committee on January 6, 1987, to investigate Iran/Contra, and the House created its Select Committee on January 7.

Congressmen and Senators immediately began declaring North's guilt at press conferences. Day after day newspapers, news magazines, and radio and television news programs repeated the declarations of his guilt by politicians. He was repeatedly accused of treason against the United States. In general he was branded a felon.

Herein lies the great political irony. If anyone was violating the Constitution, it was Congress. They were already usurping the President's constitutional power to control foreign policy. And beginning in December 1986 and January 1987, Congress's dominant faction launched a full court press to brand North as a criminal who had violated the Constitution and laws of the United States. The leadership of both houses of Congress began a process of attainting Oliver North in direct violation of Article 1, Section 9, Clause 3 of the United States Constitution.[1]

The most flagrant example of Congress's violating the Constitution was the televised kangaroo trial of North and others in the summer of 1987. The Constitution prohibits Congress from holding such hearings. *Legislative show trials are unconstitutional as bills of attainder.*[2] Simply put, Congress cannot use political trials to smear the reputations of any citizen without directly violating Article 1, Section 9, Clause 3. Legislators who conduct such procedures deserve to be impeached.

Political trials to attaint citizens make republican government impossible. Such trials deny due process, usurp and corrupt the ordinary course of justice through the courts, and make a mockery of the American system of government. Our Founding Fathers viewed the attainting of citizens through political trials as the very definition of despotism and arbitrary rule. This was the evil faced by Oliver North: he was wrongly accused of violating the Constitution by a lawless faction of Congress which would trample even on the Constitution to gain political advantage.[3]

THREE

A Government of Laws and Not of Men:
The Genius of a "Written" Constitution

A "written" Constitution. What a powerful and remarkable accomplishment! We cannot be grateful enough to our Founding Fathers for what they gave us. Because of them, and the blessing of Almighty God, the United States became the first enduring modern nation to have a "written" Constitution. How right they were to put "He has blessed our undertaking" on the Great Seal.

The word "constitution" is from the Latin *constitutio,* meaning "it is settled." When our forebears gave us a written constitution, they settled a number of basic questions about self-government among free people. Those basics can only be altered or changed by the tedious process of amendment.

In human terms, the Constitution is the "supreme law of the land." All laws and treaties must be made in harmony with it to be valid. Actions contrary to it by the Congress, the President, or the Supreme Court are void.

Our Founding Fathers were men of remarkable wisdom, experience, and learning. They did not succeed in settling all questions, slavery being one of them. But for the ones they did settle, they barely left a stone unturned. Their speeches and writings show that they tried to take into account the accumulated wisdom of the ages in order to construct our form of government.

They gave particular attention to the struggle for rights and liberties in England in the centuries following the Magna Carta (1215 A.D.). In their own contest with England, starting in 1765 and culminating in the Declaration of Independence in 1776, they took a stand for the rights of the individual person and against unjust government.

They had a very simple goal when they wrote the Constitution. They wanted to form a government of laws and not of men. On the Great Seal they phrased it with the Latin words *novus ordo seclorum*, meaning "a new order among the ages," or a new way of governing.

This simply meant that they tried to write a Constitution that would carry into effect the philosophy of the Declaration of Independence. In the Declaration, Thomas Jefferson wrote that "all men are created equal and are endowed by their Creator with certain inalienable rights." "To secure those rights," he continued, "governments are instituted among men..."

The drafters believed that liberty was a gift of God. With the Constitution they hoped to "secure the blessings of liberty," to institute a government that would secure their God-given "inalienable" rights.

The Mind of the Founders

The *Federalist Papers* written by John Jay, James Madison, and Alexander Hamilton give us a window to the minds of the Founding Fathers. John Jay was the first Chief Justice of the United States Supreme Court. James Madison was the Father of the Constitution. Alexander Hamilton was the military secretary to George Washington, the first Secretary of the Treasury, and the hero of the Battle of Yorktown. They wrote the Federalist Papers to explain the meaning of the U.S. Constitution, and to argue for its ratification by the early states.

One clear theme from the *Federalist Papers* is this: our ancestors intended America to be a country where the British system's failures to protect men's rights would be corrected, where the British system's abuses would not be repeated, and where the age-old practice of government by arbitrary power in the hands of an ambitious elite or favored faction is eliminated.

There were many such abuses to be corrected. To start with, the British had not enforced the colonists' rights as Englishmen under the common law. The powerful elite often tried to shrink the definition of particular rights so that they existed only on paper or in someone's imagination, but had no reality in daily life.

Second, the British system itself was founded on a number of principles which tended to arbitrary rule. One such principle was the notion of *parliamentary supremacy*. Since there was no written constitution in England, any law passed by parliament was the supreme law of the land, even if it conflicted with the king's promises, royal charters, bills of rights, or the common law. *Parliamentary supremacy* meant that the legislature could pass any law that it wished and violate the rights of any person.

Another flaw was the lack of separation of powers. The legislature had its own court system, the High Court of Parliament. The king had the Court of Star Chamber, which Parliament later came to dominate. Legislative, executive, and judicial powers often overlapped. Those who had obtained power often held onto it ruthlessly with cruel punishments and threats against those who were not part of the inner circle.

Our Founders wanted a government that would not be subject to the whims and caprice of ambitious men. They wanted a government where the limits of power would be clear, and where the safety and security of the citizen would be paramount.

In most other countries the king's word was law. But our forebears wanted a country where the law was king. In America, every legislator, judge, governor, and president would answer to the higher law of the Constitution. America would be a government of laws, and not of men. Justice would not depend on the whim of a legislator, a judge, or on a shifting political majority.

What they gave us wasn't perfect, and still isn't. But it was better than anything seen before or since outside the American experience. Our government, woven as it is from a combination of a "written" federal constitution and "written" state constitutions, is a work of statesmanship and genius that cannot be overstated.

FOUR

The Separation of Powers:
Did Oliver North Violate the Constitution?

When Oliver North became a Marine, he took an oath. In that oath he swore to defend the United States "against all enemies foreign and domestic." That was what he was doing when he took shrapnel in his lungs in Viet Nam and nearly died as the blood flowed from his mouth and ears.

In that oath he swore to defend to the death the Constitution of the United States. That was his "day job" as a Marine. That was also his day job for the National Security Council and the President.

There is no greater insult to a patriot than to accuse him of violating, offending, or neglecting the Constitution. There is no greater insult to a Marine than to accuse him of breaking faith with his Country, the Corps, or his oath. There is no greater insult to the American fighting man than to question his patriotism or to accuse him of treason.

But this is what was done to Oliver North by the President's political opposition and the friends of the Sandinista communists. It is unfashionable in our liberal age to point out that people have died for smaller insults. The accusations continue to this day.

No Parliamentary Supremacy

One change our Constitution made after independence from England was to put an end to parliamentary supremacy. In America, the legislature is not supreme, the Constitution is. Laws passed by Congress are only effective if they are in harmony with the Constitution.

In America, the President and the Supreme Court serve as checks and balances on Congress. The Supreme Court can declare a law of Congress void. The President can veto bills of Congress so that they do not become law. If he signs a bill into law, he has the constitutional authority and duty to *interpret the law for himself* and to *enforce the law in a way which he believes is in harmony with the Constitution.*

He may disagree with Congress on his view of what a law means or how it should be enforced. When this happens what should the President do? In America we do not have "advisory opinions" by the Supreme Court. The President cannot use the Supreme Court as his law firm. *The President has an independent constitutional duty to interpret and apply the Constitution and laws of the United States.*

He should not simply rubber stamp the opinions of the Supreme Court. He should not simply apply Congress's laws in a rote fashion. He is to "faithfully" execute the laws, that is, he must do his best to enforce them in harmony with the Constitution and in the best interests of America. If the American people disagree with how he interprets or enforces a law, they can vote him out of office. If the Congress disagrees, it can impeach him.

The President and Foreign Policy

Since the presidency of George Washington, it has been accepted that the Constitution vests foreign policy primarily in the executive branch, in the hands of the President. This is because America has equivalent foreign policy powers with the heads of state of foreign countries. The President more than Congress exercises that power for the nation. The Boland Amendments, at the core of the Iran/Contra matter, were Congress's attempt to take part of the President's foreign policy power away from him.

Article 2 of the Constitution makes the president the "commander in chief." It also vests him with the "executive power" to conduct the day-to-day business of foreign relations. The amount of history, literature, and case opinions on this issue is enormous.

When the Framers wrote the Constitution, they assumed that people would understand the principles of international law and understand the attributes of international sovereignty and executive power in sovereign states. Therefore, they did not spell them out in detail in the Constitution as if it were to be viewed as some complex legal code. John Marshall explained in McCulloch v. Maryland (1819) why such details are not spelled out in the Constitution.

John Marshall was George Washington's friend, biographer, and veteran of the frozen winter at Valley Forge. He was a famous Virginia patriot, and is numbered among the Founding Fathers. He was also a Chief Justice of the United States Supreme Court.

Marshall explained that the Constitution names areas of power and grants of authority. It uses terms that stand for large principles. The details are not defined in the document itself. We have to be familiar with the sources relied upon by the Founders to know what those grants entailed. Congress ignored those sources with the Boland Amendments and during the Iran/Contra hearings.

Cohen and Varat, in their ninth edition casebook on Constitutional Law (1993) make a helpful explanation along these lines.

> Since the primary purpose of the Founding Fathers was "to form a more perfect Union" with a stronger national government, one might suppose that the national powers over foreign affairs would have been quite fully and explicitly stated. But such was not the case. The constitutional provisions dealing expressly with foreign relations, or matters particularly related thereto, are rather sparse and uncorrelated. *Most of them appear in the enumeration of executive powers*: the President is made "Commander-in-Chief" of the armed forces; he is given the power, with the approval of two-thirds of the Senate, "to make Treaties"; and with the "advice and consent" of the Senate, he "shall appoint Ambassadors, other public Ministers and Consuls," i.e., our representatives abroad (Art. II, § 2). Also, "he shall receive

Ambassadors and other public Ministers" (Art. II. § 3). There are two additional provisions (not referring particularly to foreign affairs) under which the President has extensive undefined power. They provide "the executive power shall be vested in" him (Art. II. § 1) and "he shall take care that the Laws be faithfully executed" (Art. II. § 3).[4]

Two prime examples of the application of international law principles of sovereignty and executive power within the framework of Article 2 are Thomas Jefferson's Louisiana Purchase, and Abraham Lincoln's Emancipation Proclamation. Other examples of such exercise of executive power are abundant throughout the history of our country.

No Congressional Supremacy

I said above that the Founders did away with the notion of parliamentary supremacy. But many people seem to think otherwise. They have the overly simplistic view that the president's only power is to enforce laws which Congress has made. If that were true, the Confederates would be right that Abraham Lincoln was a tyrant.

But as James Madison explained in Federalist Paper No. 47, the division of powers is not that simple. It is not enough to say that the nation's policies are set by the legislature and carried out by the executive. Cohen & Varat point out that "Even the casual student of American history knows that the reality of the division of authority between the President and Congress has been much more complex."[5]

What the Supreme Court Has Said

Article 2 grants foreign affairs powers to the president even if Congress has not passed any corresponding laws. This is a settled principle of constitutional law. The president can act on the basis of Article 2 alone, even in the absence of relevant legislation.

Presidents have acted this way literally thousands of times. In the unhappy event that a particular piece of legislation tries to take away the president's foreign policy powers, he is not obliged to submit to such legislation.

The Supreme Court explained its views of the president's foreign policy powers in the 1936 case, U.S. v Curtiss Wright.

> ...the very delicate, plenary and exclusive power of the President as the sole organ of the Federal government in the field of international relations—a power which does not require as a basis for its exercise an act of Congress, but which, of course, like every other governmental power, must be exercised in subordination to the applicable provisions of the Constitution. It is quite apparent that if, in the maintenance of our international relations, embarrassment—perhaps serious embarrassment—is to be avoided and success for our aims achieved, congressional legislation which is to be made effective through

negotiation and inquiry within the international field must often accord to the President *a degree of discretion and freedom from statutory restriction* which would not be admissible were domestic affairs alone involved. Moreover, he, not Congress, has the better opportunity of knowing the conditions which prevail in foreign countries, and especially is this true in time of war. He has his confidential sources of information. He has his agents in the form of diplomatic, consular and other officials. *Secrecy in respect of information gathered by them may be highly necessary, and the premature disclosure of it productive of harmful results.* Indeed, so clearly is this true that the first President refused to accede to a request to lay before the House of Representatives the instructions, correspondence and documents relating to the negotiation of the Jay Treaty–a refusal the wisdom of which was recognized by the House itself and has never since been doubted. [U.S. v Curtiss-Wright Export Corp., 299 U.S. 304, 320 (1936). Emphasis added.]

In the above quote, the Court recalls the instance in which George Washington refused to turn over certain crucial information to the Congress, even though it concerned the negotiation of a treaty which would require the advice and consent of the Senate. They did not try to impeach Washington or make him out to be a criminal. Nor did they demonize his subordinates.

Similarly, it is not unquestionably clear that the Congress had a constitutional right to the information which they tried to force North to divulge. And if they did, there is a valid question of whether they were trying to cause him to disclose it prematurely.

In constitutional terms, he may not have had a duty to divulge it immediately under those circumstances. But he did have a duty to the President to protect such information. And he had a duty to foreign operatives, agents, and friends of the U.S., to keep the president's promises to them and not to put their lives and sources at risk.

One of the problems faced by North was the sheer number of various laws passed by Congress. Congress has passed volumes of laws imposing contradictory duties. Added to that was the duties imposed upon him by standing Executive Orders. North had to traverse the minefield of conflicting laws and contradictory duties at his own peril.

Disregarding Valid Legislation

Another constitutional principle which has been overlooked is that ***there are times when a president, under Article 2, may constitutionally disregard even valid legislation***. As Chief Justice Taft pointed out in 1928 in Hampton v. United States,

> The Federal Constitution and state Constitutions of this country divide the governmental power into three branches.... This is not to say that the three branches are not co-ordinate parts of one government and that each

> in the field of its duties may not invoke the action of the two other branches in so far as the action invoked shall not be an assumption of the constitutional field of action of the other branch. In determining what it may do in seeking assistance from another branch, the extent and character of that assistance must be fixed according to common sense and the inherent necessities of governmental co-ordination.[6]

With the Boland Amendments, the Congress was trying to dictate what the President's foreign policy should be with respect to Nicaragua and the Contras. This was an intrusion into the constitutional field of another branch.

Common sense and the necessities inherent in the co-ordination or lack of co-ordination are valid considerations in the president's exercise of his direct Article 2 powers. This is the President's call under our Constitution! There are times when the President, exercising his own judgment in assessing his duties in light of present necessities, can act in international affairs in contravention of congressional policy and may even disregard valid laws.

Doing so is not automatically a high crime or misdemeanor because of the nature and scope of executive authority as a co-ordinate branch. The key is whether the President is acting pursuant to a legitimate constitutional end. If that is the case, any means which are consistent with the letter and spirit of the constitution are constitutional. This is supposed to be a political question rather than a legal question. It is supposed to be resolved at the ballot box rather than before the jury box.

No Violation of the Constitution

Because our Constitution places the control of foreign policy in the hands of the President, and because Oliver North was carrying out the policies of the president, *he did not violate the United States Constitution*. Nothing in that policy was contrary to the letter or spirit of the U.S. Constitution.

Indeed, the President was faced with the insane dilemma of trying to defend democracy and aid the victims of despotism in Nicaragua while the majority party in Congress was walking arm in arm with a communist dictatorship that was colonizing the western hemisphere in flagrant defiance of the Monroe doctrine.

Added to that outrage was the fact that Congress tried to make criminal a *policy difference* between the legislative branch and executive branch. They wanted to neuter and domesticate the Reagan White House. That is the sole reason for which they undertook the Iran/Contra witchhunt.

If Oliver North violated the Constitution, then so did FDR, when he ignored neutrality legislation and secretly supplied aid to Britain and France against the Nazis prior to Pearl Harbor. If North's accusers are right in the principle which they assert, then the list of executive branch criminals would start with George Washington, end with George Bush, and would include Lincoln, FDR, Truman, and many others.

FIVE

Bill of Attainder

How Congress Violated the Constitution In its Treatment of Oliver North, et al.

Why did we have the American Revolution in the first place? One reason, among many, was that the colonists were outraged by political show trials, *the same kind of political trial used to attaint Oliver North and others.*

In the catalog of abuses which the King and Parliament visited upon our country's founders, one which our Founders denounce repeatedly in their writings is that of "attainder," *where the legislature smears an enemy of the political majority by holding a public hearing, making him the target of accusations.*

The goal of an attainder hearing is to "attaint" or brand a man with perpetual disgrace, to ruin his reputation, to make him odious – to convince the public that he is a threat to the common good and that he should be expelled from political life.

In medieval times, because the King and Parliament wielded the kinds of unrestrained power which our founders condemned, often the victim was actually physically branded. He might be forced to have his nose slit as a punishment. Or he might be physically mutilated or tortured in other ways. The government could take all his lands and goods, make him unemployable, and put an end to all his civil rights. During that period of English history, people were put to death for the so-called "crime" of merely disagreeing with the ruling party.

If legislators wished to target a political enemy, they could hold a public trial and make sure that everyone in the land knew that this man was suspected and accused. *They had the unilateral power to make his actions criminal regardless of what those actions were.* They would simply redefine the law.

They would force him to testify against himself. If he refused to incriminate himself, they could jail (and torture) him for contempt. And, at the end, they would publish a bill containing the accusations and conclusions of guilt.

If the punishment was death, it was called a "bill of attainder." If the punishment was something less, such as physical torture or life imprisonment, it was called a "bill of pains and penalties."

Over the course of time, the term "bill of attainder" came to include both attainder and pains and penalties. In early America, the term "bill of attainder" applied to a *legislative hearing* where the goal was to *defame a man's character and ruin his reputation,* regardless of what other punishments were inflicted on him. The attainting process is a serious threat to liberty for one simple reason, <u>it almost always works</u>!

Not in America, You Don't!

Our American ancestors despised political trials so much that they placed <u>two</u> prohibitions against bills of attainder in the U.S. Constitution. *Long before they added the Bill of Rights, they barred Congress from using public hearings as a pretext to pursue a political vendetta against any citizen.* Putting an end to attainders as an engine of political persecution was one of their foremost political concerns.

This fact is vital. Why was "no bills of attainder" so important to our Founding Fathers from the very first? Why not free speech? Why not free press? Why not free exercise of religion? Why not the right to keep and bear arms? Constitutional protection for these rights came later.

The answer is simple. Legislative show trials make constitutional self-government an illusion. Liberty and justice for all becomes a joke. Legislators who instigate and conduct political trials spit on the graves of the martyrs of the American Revolution. When legislatures hold political trials, the American Revolution is lost.

Attainder hearings are dangerous to liberty. They destroy the separation of powers. They paralyze the system of checks and balances. They entrench the politically powerful. And they stigmatize any part of the community that rises to defend the person who is the object of the attack. Attainder hearings are a cancer to the republican form of government.

Our forefathers knew that political trials had a very simple goal: *to divide* the community by inflaming its passions, *to isolate* one's political opponents and neutralize their popular support, and *to enlarge* and solidify the elite's hold over the majority of the community. Tyranny can be very effective.

"No bills of attainder" is hardly a passionate rallying cry of modern civil libertarians. It should be, especially in light of how successful Congress was in 1987 of attainting Oliver North in the eyes of so many people. Today, however, when people passionately defend our "constitutional" rights as Americans, seldom if ever do we include "no bills of attainder" in the list. We usually emphasize free speech, free press, and other rights named in the Bill of Rights, which were added to the Constitution *later.*

During the hearings in the summer of 1987, we were deluged with experts – lawyers, sociologists, political commentators, and politicians of every stripe. Every major news organization in the country had its best and most brilliant minds working on analyzing and dissecting the Iran/Contra hearings. But not once, to my knowledge, did the legal experts and media commentators suggest that the hearings might be violating the prohibition against bills of attainder.

The real story in the summer of 1987 was that Congress itself trashed the Constitution with an attainder hearing. That story was not covered then, and has not been covered since. The gimmick worked and Congress got away with it.

Many people who would fight to the death to protect the rights of free speech or free press against governmental encroachment, are the very same ones who deride Oliver North as a criminal based on the televised hearings in the summer of 1987. *They do not know that they have fallen for the age-old legislative trick of redefining the law to attaint and ruin a person whom the legislature finds to be a political nuisance.*

SIX

To Impeach or Not to Impeach

Congress's Dirty Little Secret

Being short on time means I can get right to the point. It is this. Congress wanted to impeach Reagan, but didn't dare try. He was much too popular, loved, and respected. So they went on a fishing expedition, using an illegal political trial, to try to accomplish the same result without having to admit it. Their dilemma – how to depose or at least debilitate the chief executive without making a lot of voters furious.

The solution, of course, was to try to convince the voting public that the President, or at least the President's men, had committed high crimes and misdemeanors. This would be grounds for impeachment. To accomplish this goal, they had to convince the public that it was somehow a criminal offense for the President to carry out his chosen foreign policy.

Never mind that this meant that the Congress was trying to take over the White House. Never mind that they were trying to tell this president that he did not have the same powers exercised by every president before him since George Washington. Never mind that they were creating a Congressiocracy in defiance of the Constitution's mandated balance of powers. Why let a little thing like Article 2 of the U.S. Constitution stand in the way of the political aggrandizement of certain powerful legislators and their party?

By All Means Don't Use the "I" Word

Yes, the president's opponents in Congress had a dirty little secret. They desperately longed to impeach Reagan, to emasculate his administration, to humble him and eviscerate his leadership. But they couldn't use the "I" word, they couldn't talk of impeachment without risking a backlash from the public. They would have to wait.

In the meantime, they had this marvelous opportunity. Lower employees in the executive branch were caught carrying out a policy which Congress opposed. If Congress could put enough pressure on those subordinates, especially with threats of jail time or prison, somebody would crack under the pressure and blame the president. All Congress needed to do was to turn up the pressure on the president's men, and in due time, the president would be handed to them like John the Baptist's head on a platter.

So Congress baited the trap and began looking for someone who would be a Judas. They needed to find someone who had the most to lose and the least to gain by staying faithful to the president. It is a human trait, you know, to betray your friends to save your own skin, especially if they have already betrayed you.

Who fit the description better than Oliver North? He was at the bottom of the totem pole in the President's circle. He was a worker bee for the National Security Council, headed by Robert McFarlane. He was a Marine, taking orders from above, including ancillary links to William Casey, the head of the CIA.

North was the perfect fall guy – for both sides. He was expendable to the White House and the intelligence services, and he was a convenient pawn for Congress. He had the most to lose.

He had spent his entire life as a "can do" Marine. He was not a professional politician or a top level decision maker in the executive branch. But he had risen to the coveted rank of Lieutenant Colonel. He had served directly under the President of the United States. In a few years he would be eligible for full retirement.

Congress thought they had their man. North was obviously a facilitator of covert operations and policy. He knew operational details and facts. If he took the blame upon himself to protect the president, he could lose all that he had worked for. He could lose his retirement, he could go to prison, he could be thrown out of the Corps. He could lose it all.

Soldiers aren't rich. It would be impossible for him to bankroll the coterie of lawyers needed to defend himself against Congress's onslaught or the inevitable criminal trial. He would be no match financially for the unlimited money resources in the hands of his political persecutors. It would not be a fair fight. They had him surrounded. He would be forced to surrender. He would have to hang out the white flag.

After all, he had already been selected by the White House to be the scapegoat. Consequently, his sense of duty should be at an all time low. He of all people had the most to lose and every reason to save his own skin. Congress was certain that they had their man. Surely he would roll over on the president. But they failed to keep in mind the simple lesson that so many have learned the hard way – never underestimate a Marine.

Impeachment by any Other Name is... "Congressional Oversight"

The political trial of Oliver North did not start out simply as a vendetta against him. He was a means to an end – a pawn. Congress wanted to use him to get to the President. North was supposed to give them the commander in chief. They expected North to testify in a self-serving way, to exonerate himself at the President's expense. Once North provided the crucial links between Reagan and the Contra aid, Congress could impeach Reagan. That was the script.

North did not follow the script. At first he refused to testify at all, relying on the cherished Fifth Amendment right against self-incrimination. But Congress has found a way to get around the Fifth Amendment. They "grant immunity," meaning that one <u>must</u> testify or go to jail for contempt. Theoretically, whatever one says under "immunity" cannot be used against him in a court of law.

So Congress "immunized" North and forced him to testify. It was no big deal to them, because the grant of immunity was hollow, and North was only a means to an end. They wanted Reagan. Keep in mind that their goal was to demolish the Reagan presidency.

Congress had been working on staging the drama for over six months. They had been gathering testimony, interviewing witnesses, examining documents, and making appropriate "leaks" to the media. Nothing was left to chance. They had extracted "confessions" from a few who knew that they were powerless to oppose Congress. The foundation was already carefully laid.

After half a year of preparation, it was time to spring the trap. The hot lights and television cameras were in place. The vulturous grins on the faces of the inquisitors, awaiting the appearance of the accused in their lair, told the whole story. They were absolutely certain that when Oliver North sat down at the table to testify before the select committees, he would say the magic words "Ronald Reagan made me do it." North would walk free. And Reagan would be theirs.

When You're Right Stand and Fight

The lieutenant colonel strode into the room, his face like flint and a defiant fire in his eyes. Smirking faces, some distinctly resembling the salivating wolves from Little Red Riding Hood cartoons, peered down self-righteous noses at him. They started the inquisition by proclaiming his guilt, one of their many violations of the Constitution and of due process.

Then they refused to allow him to make his opening statement, which called into question the constitutional and legal grounds for the hearing. They dare not let the American public hear that statement or allow the media to analyze it and respond to it. Why? Because then the American sense of fair play would swing in his favor, and Congress would look like the bully that it was. They had to shut him up. So they did, and proceeded with the inquisition.

But to their amazement, they faced a man with no fear. He did not fold. He did not shrink. He did not try to save himself. He looked them in the eye.

The showdown was to have been shorter than the Battle of Bull Run, and end with North in swift retreat. But their smirking smiles turned to gloom when he would not give them Reagan to save himself, and he would not kiss their rings either. What was to be a rout bogged down into a trench warfare stalemate, as North repelled assault after assault. More outnumbered than Custer at the Little Big Horn, he held them at bay for six days.

When they realized that he would not give them Reagan, North himself became their primary target. There was only one problem. They had granted him immunity. All they could do now to punish him was to do their best to ruin his reputation and his future – to attaint *him*. That's why they all but tarred and feathered him. Nothing compares to the wrath of a Congress scorned. But they had blundered greatly. By miscalculating they had lost the President and North.

SEVEN

A Ruse is a Ruse is a Ruse

More of How Congress Violated the Constitution With a Covert Impeachment Strategy

Impeachment by any other name is, in a word, unconstitutional. The select committees' televised hearings in the summer of 1987 were impeachment hearings, thinly disguised.

In addition to violating the constitutional separation of powers between the legislative and executive branches, in addition to violating the Constitution's prohibition against bills of attainder, Congress's select committees and televised hearings also *violated the separation of powers between the legislature and the judiciary*, and *violated the Constitution's rules for impeachments*. Here's why.

One of the worst nightmares for the American colonists was in having to deal with Parliament. Because of the lack of separation of powers in England, Parliament not only had legislative powers, it also exercised judicial powers. When the colonists tried to defend their rights, sometimes it was before the "high court of Parliament."

This meant that when the Founders went to the "highest court" to defend their rights which were being denied by Parliament's unjust laws, *the judges were the same people who had passed those laws in the first place*. Justice was impossible in that situation because the wrongdoer was also the judge. To be a judge in one's own cause violates the first principles of due process.

The Parliament could also use what is called the *inquisitorial* method of trial, a European practice which was rejected by our Founding Fathers. It differs from the *adversarial* method used in American law courts where two opposing sides argue their case before an impartial judge. *The inquisitorial method allows the judge to act also as a prosecuting attorney. The judge is the other side. And he may ask any question of the accused on any subject whatsoever.*

To correct this problem, our Founders decided to separate the legislative and judicial powers, and to ban the *inquisitorial* method from American courts. They granted certain legislative powers to Congress. And they vested almost all judicial powers in the Supreme Court.

There were a few limited exceptions. Congress was given judicial power (1) to judge the elections, returns, and qualifications of its own members, (2) to punish its members for disorderly behavior or expel a member, and (3) to impeach public officers for treason, bribery, or other high crimes and misdemeanors. If Congress acts like a court in other situations, it violates the Constitution and the separation of powers.

The Constitution and Impeachment

The word *impeach* means to accuse. It is similar to the word *indict*. The words differ in that an indictment is a formal accusation of criminal charges which are tried in a court of law. An impeachment formally accuses a public officer of conduct which violates the public trust.[7] The trial is conducted by the legislature.

The rules about impeachments are very strict. The Constitution directs that *only the House of Representatives may bring articles of impeachment,* the formal accusations of wrongdoing.[8] When the House of Representatives has investigated and drawn up formal charges, it presents those charges to the Senate. *The Senate has the sole power to sit as a court to try all impeachments.*[9]

If a government official has committed an impeachable offense, the House alone must investigate and bring the charge. The Senate cannot be involved. When the Senate sits to determine guilt or innocence the House cannot participate in the trial. *The two houses cannot be mixed as was done in the 1987 hearings.* The combined panel of senators and congressmen who grilled Oliver North violated the plain terms of the U.S. Constitution.[10]

Congress's Investigative Power

The power to investigate and to accuse varies greatly between the legislative and judicial branches of government. In criminal investigations before the judicial branch, the *prosecutorial method* is used in an accusing, adversarial way because *the accused has the protections of due process, the rules of evidence and procedure, and the presumptions of innocence, etc.* Plus, the judge is not a party to the dispute. He can judge fairly between the two parties because he has no personal stake in the matter.

In the legislature, on the other hand, these rules do not apply to protect someone who is accused. Therefore the legislature's power to investigate is narrowly limited to finding out whether more legislation is needed to guide public officials in how to carry out their appointed tasks under the Constitution and laws of the United States. *The goal is to identify whether there is a need for additional legislation.*

The only instance where a congressional investigation can use the prosecutorial style of accusing and making charges of wrongdoing is when the House of Representatives is in the process of bringing an impeachment. Otherwise, prosecutorial hearings in Congress to establish someone's guilt are unconstitutional. Where impeachments are concerned, the inquisitorial method of interrogating witnesses is banned entirely.

It is very clear from the televised hearings of 1987 that the committee, made up of both congressmen and senators, was conducting an inquisition to find out if someone – anyone – in the executive branch had violated some law. This was not simply a hearing to identify whether there was a need for additional legislation.

This was a clearly a prosecutorial trial to establish guilty acts. As such it violated the separation of powers between the legislature and the judiciary. Ostensibly, it was an "oversight" hearing. But the announced purpose was merely a pretext, a disguise, for the true underlying purpose – *to impeach and attaint members of the executive branch*. Congress even granted immunity to certain witnesses, which ordinarily is the prerogative of the special counsel who *by Congress's law is an officer of the judicial branch.*

Had Congress obeyed the Constitution, the House of Representatives would have conducted the investigation and then laid the articles of impeachment before the Senate. But in the Iran/Contra inquisition the Senate was involved from the very beginning, in clear violation of the requirements of the United States Constitution.

Had Congress obeyed the Constitution, the Senate would have conducted the trial to determine guilt or innocence. But the Iran/Contra inquisition was prosecuted before a combined panel of senators and representatives, in clear violation of the Constitution's requirement that the Senate alone must conduct the impeachment trial.

Since an impeachment trial is a judicial proceeding, even though it occurs in the halls of the legislature, the ordinary rules of due process are supposed to apply. The select committee claimed that those rules did not apply to Oliver North because they denied that they were conducting an impeachment hearing. But a rose by any other name is still a rose.

If this was not an impeachment trial, then Congress lacked the authority to act in a *prosecutorial* manner. Regardless of what kind of trial it was, their *inquisitorial* style was unconstitutional from the outset. But this was an impeachment trial. And the judges were not impartial, they had a personal stake in the dispute. They were, in effect, the "high court of Parliament" revisited.

Alexander Hamilton, in Federalist Paper 65, explained the purpose of impeachment trials with these words: "[T]he trial of impeachments (is for) those offenses which proceed . . . from the abuse or violation of some public trust." This is what distinguishes impeachment proceedings from other legislative hearings.

When Senator Daniel Inouye, the Senate chairman of select committee, opened the hearings he said: "These hearings . . . will examine what happens when the trust that is the lubricant of our system is breached by high officials in our government." These words of the chairman expose the fact that this was indeed an impeachment hearing, plain and simple.

Congress professed to be holding an oversight hearing, but their words and conduct indicated otherwise. The announced purpose was merely a pretext, a ruse, to impeach members of the executive branch. What we beheld was impeachment by sleight of hand, violating every rule in the Constitution on how impeachments are to be carried out.

By July 27, 1987, after ten weeks of hearings, the Washington Post reported that the hearings had been so unproductive from Congress's viewpoint that there probably would not be an impeachment of Reagan.

EIGHT

The Boland Amendments

Making the World Safe for Communism

Because Congress was so successful in attainting Oliver North in the summer of 1987, large numbers of people still believe the myth that he somehow violated the Boland Amendments by helping the Nicaraguan Contras. There was no violation.

The Boland Amendments were spending restrictions added to appropriations bills. They applied to U.S. Government appropriated funds – funds drawn from the U.S. Treasury. Such funds were never used by Oliver North. The Boland Amendments had no bearing on any of his Contra aid activities.

Background

The Boland Amendments were Congress's attempt to stop Reagan from helping the Contras. They were Congress's way of making the world safe for communism.

The Sandinista Communists took over Nicaragua in 1979 near the end of the failed presidency of Jimmy Carter. They immediately set up a communist dictatorship which seized lands, farms, businesses, factories, and whole industries. They shut down newspapers, squelched free speech, and had their critics assassinated.

The Sandinistas seized the territorial homelands of the Miskito Indians who had been Christianized by protestant missionaries. Hundreds of pastors were jailed in "tiger cages," pits dug in the ground, having bars across the top. The Christian ministers were completely exposed to the rain and elements. They had only enough room to turn around. When they were fed, the food was lowered through the bars just above their heads at ground level.

Women, young and old, were raped by the military after being forced to watch their fathers, husbands, sons, or brothers being executed. Sometimes as many as 1,000 people per day fled for safety to Honduras or Costa Rica. The number and description of the various atrocities were horrifying.

The Sandinista dictatorship broke all of its promises to hold elections, preserve human rights and political liberties, and to uphold the charter of the Organization of the American States. The Sandinistas allied themselves with Cuba and with the communist faction which later seized the island of Grenada.

Documents captured by the U.S. during the Grenada invasion revealed how the Sandinistas had joined forces with North Korea and various other communist countries, and countries involved in international terrorism. Nicaragua became the conduit through which communist governments and terrorist organizations could funnel military weapons, communications facilities, personnel, and training to communist insurgents who were trying to destabilize Nicaragua's democratic neighbors.

The Sandinistas were actively involved in seeking to overthrow the government of El Salvador and other Central America countries. Edward P. Boland was the chairman of the House Intelligence Committee which investigated and published such facts. He was also the author of the "Boland Amendments" which tried to stop President Reagan from being able to counter the illegal activities of the Sandinistas in Central America.

Boland #1

There were actually three Boland Amendments. The first one became law on December 21, 1982. It restricted the CIA or the Department of Defense from giving military aid to the Contras. These are very narrow restrictions and allowed a broad range of official activity with respect to the Nicaragua problem.

Boland #2

In 1983, Congress itself provided $24 million to the Contras. It also rewrote the Boland Amendment to say that once the $24 million was expended, no more funding could be given by the CIA, the DOD, or any other agency or entity of the U.S. *involved in intelligence activities.*[11]

In 1984, when the $24 million had been spent, Congress refused President Reagan's request for additional funds. The Boland Amendment was re-enacted unchanged.

Boland #3

In 1985, Congress again voted to deny funds to the Contras. To celebrate his victory, Sandinista dictator Daniel Ortega made a trip to Moscow. An embarrassed Congress flip-flopped and reinstated funding, but only in the form of humanitarian aid. The CIA and the DOD were prohibited from distributing the aid.

At the same time, another version of Boland was added to the appropriations act of 1985. It prohibited the CIA, the DOD, or any other agency involved in intelligence activities from giving money drawn from the U.S. Treasury to the Contras for military support.

No Boland

In October 1986, Congress appropriated $100 million to aid the Nicaraguan resistance. Congress was finally getting the picture. However, this was the same month in which the Iran/Contra matter began to be disclosed.

No Violation

The Boland Amendments were never violated. They were conditions placed on appropriations bills which mandated how American tax money would be spent or could not be spent. ***They applied only to the CIA, the DOD, and to intelligence agencies.***

They did not apply to the president directly nor to the National Security Council. The NSC was funded by executive branch appropriations, not by funding for intelligence agencies. The NSC had never been identified or included in any of congress's detailed lists naming the various parts of the intelligence community.[12] The NSC was not viewed by Congress as an intelligence agency and was not covered by the Boland Amendments.

Second, *the Boland Amendments could not and did not restrict the President's constitutional power to support the Nicaraguan Democratic Resistance,* in any manner other that stopping him from spending funds appropriated by Congress from the Treasury of the United States. This could not and did not deprive the President of his authority under the Constitution to encourage other nations to give aid, nor did it restrict private benefactors from giving aid through international channels.

We must keep in mind the fact that under the U.S. Constitution:

> [T]he President alone has the power to speak or listen as a representative of the nation.... As Marshall said in his great argument of March 7, 1800, in the House of Representatives, "The President is the sole organ of the nation in its external relations, and its sole representative with foreign nations." [Justice Sutherland, United States v. Curtiss-Wright Export Corp., (1936), unanimous opinion].
>
> The President is the Constitutional representative of the United States with regard to foreign nations. He manages our concerns with foreign nations.... The nature of transactions with foreign nations, moreover, requires caution and unity of design, and their success frequently depends on secrecy and

dispatch. [Senate Foreign Relations Committee, February 15, 1816].[13]

Furthermore, Congress knew of many of the private efforts to assist the Contras as early as 1985. [131 Cong. Record, H4118, June 12, 1985.] When a bill was introduced in 1985 to make such private aid illegal, the bill was defeated.

It is very interesting to note that when Rep. Edward Boland himself interrogated Adm. Poindexter in July 1987, *he could not identify a single specific violation* of the three amendments which he himself had authored.

Boland's own staffers admitted that they did not know whether any of the three restrictions were violated: "We think [the latest provisions] expired in December, 1985. But we're not entirely certain."[14]

The Boland Amendment, in its various versions, did not forbid Iranian contributions to the Contras; it did not forbid private aid to the Contras; and it did not apply to the NSC staff. It was a civil statute with no criminal penalties. And it was never demonstrated that North or Poindexter violated it.

The Height of Hypocrisy

During Reagan's first four year term, the democrats did not control the U.S. Senate. Reagan was able to get some aid for the democratic resistance in Nicaragua during that time. But the democrats regained control of the Senate during his second term. During that period, the democrat majority furiously resisted every effort of Reagan to aid the Contras.

Out of necessity, Reagan had to rely on direct Article 2 powers to orchestrate aid for the Contras despite Congress's opposition.

Several months after the Iran/Contra hearings ended, the Sandinistas invaded Honduras, their democratic neighbor. This was two weeks after the final cutoff of U.S. assistance to the Contras. The democrat leadership was humiliated because this was the sort of aggression about which the Reagan administration had warned, and which many in Congress denied would ever happen.

As a consequence, President Reagan had to send two battalions of the 82d Airborne and two battalions of the 7th Infantry Division to Honduras In March 1988.

On Wednesday, March 17, 1988, the Iran-Contra indictments were finally handed down against North and Poindexter. Ironically, that very same day, democrat Tony Coelho said on the House floor that "the Republicans abandoned the Contras" and that the collapse of the Contra resistance which had kept the Sandinistas out of Honduras was the Republicans' fault!

To say that the Republicans had abandoned the Contras was the height of hypocrisy. At long last, the president's policy had been indisputably vindicated. The Sandinistas, fearing American military involvement, agreed to a cease fire on March 24. North had been right, cold comfort to a patriot facing a contrived criminal indictment against him.

NINE

Bleeding the Fifth

Congress's Attack on the Fifth Amendment

They say the road to perdition is paved with good intentions. The road to Star Chamber was. Star Chamber was one of those awful places in history where well-meaning but misguided men ruined the lives and reputations of many good and decent people. The terrible lessons learned there led our Founding Fathers to put the Fifth Amendment's right against self-incrimination in the Constitution. Star Chamber was abolished 1641. Congress revived it in 1987.

The Court of Star Chamber

Star Chamber was a beautiful room in Westminster in London. The ceiling was inlaid with ornate glass in the shape of stars. The King's Council often used the room for important meetings. It was there that the infamous Court of Star Chamber came into existence.[15]

The Court of Star Chamber started out as a place where common people could be protected from oppression by corrupt members of the nobility. But Star Chamber was not bound by the ordinary rules of the courts of law. In due time, Star Chamber ceased being part of the solution. It became part of the problem.

The flaw in Star Chamber was simple. It operated not as a law court, but as an executive council – an immensely powerful committee. It exercised vast discretionary powers. It was not bound by the rules of due process. Its power to investigate anyone on any subject was unlimited. Its prerogatives grew to be almost boundless. It had whatever authority it claimed for itself. Its declarations had the force of law.

Because it had the power to issue and enforce proclamations, the council could exercise legislative, executive, and judicial functions. In 1539 Parliament passed a law giving Star Chamber the right to legislate on any subject.

One of Star Chamber's more frightening powers was the ability to create new offenses. It imposed harsh penalties for even minor violations. The accused were subjected to trial before arbitrary tribunals which had already prejudged their guilt or innocence.

Star Chamber could subpoena any citizen to appear and force him to testify about any matter or any person. If the committee had heard any rumor or had received any complaint or accusation against a person, it would bring the accused before the council.

The accused would not be told the identity of his accuser nor the crime for which he was accused. Rather, he would be placed under oath and commanded to testify. He was required to answer any question asked of him. If he refused to answer, he would be placed in prison.

The "Oath Ex Officio"

The favorite tool of Star Chamber was the "*oath ex officio*." Every person brought before the council to answer questions was first placed under oath. This allowed the questioners to treat every lapse of memory, any nervously scrambled sentence, or any recollection which differed slightly from that of another witness as intentional lying and the crime of perjury. To be human and to testify under oath guaranteed that the accused could be turned into a criminal.

The accused could be required to answer questions on any subject, no matter how incriminating. The accused could be forced to testify against his family, friends, or acquaintances. The committee could "create" criminals by cutting and pasting the testimony of various witnesses and imagining some sinister conspiracy because of minor differences in testimony.

No one was safe, no matter how hard one tried to cooperate with the committee. It is a fact of human existence that everyone's memory fails to some degree, and differs with that of others to some degree.

Since every witness would have another who disagreed to some extent, or who remembered differently to some extent, every witness could be made to appear to be "hiding something," "giving misleading answers," or of "answering falsely."

The procedures and assumptions used by Star Chamber were designed to ensnare people rather than to find the truth. And it was a favorite practice of Star

Chamber to force a man to testify in such a way as to ensnare his friends in order to save himself.

When John Lilburne was tried in 1637, he was willing to answer questions concerning charges made against him. He denied the charges and objected to being forced to incriminate himself. But when he was ordered to testify against others he said:

> I am not willing to answer you to any more of these questions, because I see you go about this Examination to ensnare me; for seeing the things for which I am imprisoned cannot be proved against me, you will get other matter out of my examination; and therefore if you will not ask me about the thing laid to my charge, I shall answer no more.[16]

Lilburne was set in the pillory and tortured.

Star Chamber and the Fifth Amendment

Star Chamber was abolished in 1641. Over the next 25 years in England, a great public debate took place concerning the ability of English courts and commissions to force people to testify. During the civil war in the 1640s, great progress was made toward ending the use of the "oath ex officio" and of the practice even in law courts of causing the accused to incriminate themselves.

The Court of Star Chamber was restored for a brief time under Charles II in the 1660s. But even then the inquisitorial, unlimited investigative powers of the council were not restored. By that time it had become settled that no officer, judge, or council member could require any person to testify to any matter whereby he might be incriminated. This privilege was also extended to the common law courts.

The abolition of Star Chamber put an end to the inquisitorial method of hearings and trials in England. It required instead the use of the adversarial method and the safeguards of judicial due process. Abolishing Star Chamber opened the way to the establishment of the privilege against self-incrimination.[17]

Our ancestors valued that privilege so highly that they wrote it into the Constitution of the United States and the bills of rights of every state. The Fifth Amendment in the Bill of Rights reads: "No person shall be . . . compelled, in any criminal case, to be witness against himself; . . ."

1987: Star Chamber Restored

The Iran/Contra investigation, televised hearings, and subsequent criminal prosecutions ominously parallel the ancient abuses of Star Chamber. Congress itself passed the laws and made the pronouncements which set the stage for this terrible abuse of power. Part of this abuse came from the arbitrary and unrestrained power delegated by Congress to the Office of Independent Counsel, which conducted a seven year vendetta to persecute Oliver North and others who were accused.

From the beginning the Iran/Contra witchhunt was a direct assault on the Fifth Amendment. Before and during the hearings in the summer of 1987, numerous congressmen and senators reviled North and others for asserting their fifth amendment right against self-incrimination.

North's unwillingness to "incriminate himself" on matters which were never crimes in the first place was used by the Select Committees as proof that he was a criminal. Their proof that he was a criminal lay in the fact that he refused to confess that he was a criminal! The Court of Star Chamber was now in session!

Like Star Chamber, Congress had created new offenses whereby to trap their political enemies. More on this later. North was ordered by his superiors to walk into the trap by the very act of carrying out the President's foreign policy.

The Select Committees (and the Independent Counsel) exercised vast discretionary powers and almost unlimited investigatory powers. They were not bound by the rules of due process of law. They combined legislative, executive, and judicial functions. They formed themselves into an arbitrary tribunal which had already prejudged the guilt of the persons whom they had accused. They went out of their way to ensnare the witnesses and to force them to incriminate themselves and each other. And many Americans fell for it because they did not know that the criminal actors in the drama were the dominant faction of Congress instead of the members of the executive branch.

TEN

Iran/amok

A Congress Out of Control

In Iran/Contra, Congress violated the Constitution's separation of powers between the executive branch and the legislative branch, violated the separation of powers between the legislative branch and the judicial branch, violated the Constitution's prohibition against bills of attainder, and violated the Fifth Amendment's right against self-incrimination.

Congress's own activities in Iran/Contra and the powers that it delegated to the Office of the Independent Counsel revived the abuses of the hated Court of Star Chamber. When viewed as a whole and not just as separate parts, these actions by Congress evidence an attempt on the part of the dominant faction of Congress to seize powers vested in the president by the Constitution.

Seizure of government power without right is known as a *coup d'état*. Congress's Iran/Contra drama was a type of legislative power grab, a coup of state. In the end, one man stood alone to resist that coup: Lieutenant Colonel Oliver North.[18]

Unknown to most Americans in 1987 was the fact that a constitutional crisis was playing out before our eyes. Congress was running amok. To accomplish its power grab, Congress had to trample on the Constitution and on the rights which the Constitution guarantees.

The Secret Coup

Congress Seizes Presidential Power

The key to the Iran/Contra drama is one simple concept: *parliamentary supremacy.* Our forefathers rejected the concept of parliamentary supremacy when they threw the tea in the Boston Harbor. (Remember that the Stamp Act Crisis was over a two-penny tax. It wasn't the money, it was the principle of the thing.) American independence and the Constitution of the United States put an end to parliamentary supremacy as a controlling principle of American government.

The Iran/Contra scandal came about because Congress's dominant faction returned to the principle of parliamentary supremacy rejected by our nation's forefathers. During Reagan's presidency, that faction viewed itself as supreme over the president, rather than as a co-ordinate branch of government.

Congress operated on the principle that the president *could do only what Congress had authorized him to do*. Congress legislated as though the president lacked any foreign policy powers. Congress acted as if Congress alone had the right and power to determine the foreign policy of the United States.

By passing laws requiring the president and the executive branch to enforce Congress's policy only, under threat of criminal penalties, Congress sought to dominate the White House and exercise the president's constitutional office for him. This erroneous view of the relationship between the legislative and executive branches makes the president little more than congress's puppet and a rubber stamp.

The Lawrence Walsh Show

I said above that the key to understanding the Iran/Contra drama was the principle of *parliamentary supremacy*. It is also the key to understanding the issue of criminality. *The President's support for the Contras could only be criminal if Congress is supreme over the president in foreign affairs.* Without parliamentary supremacy as a foundation, the whole notion of criminality falls apart.

That is why Lawrence Walsh, the Independent Counsel, had to adopt the idea of parliamentary supremacy to be able to pursue Oliver North with criminal charges.

SOCIETY OF COMPUTER FORENSIC INVESTIGATORS

Gary Amos, J.D., C.F.C.E.
Vice President

621 Orangewood Drive
Virginia Beach, Virginia
23453-2124

Office: 757.463.8169
Cell: 757.672.3522

> The underlying facts of Iran/contra are that . . . President Reagan, the secretary of state, the secretary of defense, and the director of central intelligence and their necessary assistants committed themselves . . . to two programs *contrary to congressional policy and contrary to national policy.*[19]

In the next sentence, Walsh concludes that by implementing a foreign policy that was different from that of Congress, Reagan and the members of his Administration broke the law. .

> They skirted the law, some of them broke the law, and almost all of them tried to cover up the President's willful activities. . . .[20]

Walsh is so convinced that Congress, and not the president, has the exclusive authority to control foreign affairs that Congress should have openly confronted the president for his "disrespect" of Congress's authority.

> The disrespect for Congress by a popular and powerful President and his appointees was obscured when congress accepted the tendered concept of a runaway conspiracy of subordinate officers and avoided the unpleasant confrontation with a powerful President and his Cabinet.[21]

Walsh says that it was President Reagan himself who was the kingpin in a conspiracy to violate the law:[22]

> [T.]he Iran/Contra affair was not an aberrational scheme carried out by a 'cabal of zealots' on the National Security Council Staff. . . . Instead, it was the product of two foreign policy directives by President Reagan which skirted the law. . . .

How did Reagan violate the law according to Walsh? "[F]rom the President's determination to support the contras" after a federal ban on their support "in the Boland Amendment in October 1984."[23]

"The tone in Iran/contra was set by President Reagan," Walsh says. "He directed that the contras be supported, despite a ban on contra aid *imposed on him by Congress*."[24]

These quotes reveal the central core of the Iran/Contra drama, Congress believed that it could dictate all foreign policy for the president, and Walsh agreed. This made any disagreement which Reagan might have with Congress a criminal offense rather than a dispute over policy!

Because Congress and the Independent Counsel embraced the unconstitutional notion of parliamentary supremacy, they elevated a policy disagreement between two co-ordinate branches of government into a constitutional crisis! Congress used the opportunity to seize presidential power, and tried to assure its own victory by using its lawmaking powers to criminalize any action taken by the President to exercise his foreign policy prerogatives under the Constitution.

Guilty by Not Breaking the Law

Maybe you did not believe me when I told you that Oliver North's persecutors could invent crimes as they went along. Maybe you did not believe that they would try to turn innocence into guilt and make a man guilty by hocus pocus.

In that case you should read volume 1 of the Walsh Report. Part three explains his legal theory of why Oliver North was a criminal. Do you have a guess of what it was? (Don't forget now, we're dealing with the Grand Inquisitor from Star Chamber.) You guessed it, Oliver North was guilty of trying NOT to violate the laws.

As ludicrous as it seems, you heard me right. (I know. I couldn't believe it either.)

Walsh explains that North was guilty of the crime of defrauding the United States by actively trying to help the Contras in a way that would not violate the law! His "criminal activity" consisted in his efforts to aid the Contras in a noncriminal way! (I told you that Star Chamber logic is bizarre.)

> Poindexter, North, and their co-conspirators carried out their "secret war" in a way calculated to defeat legal restrictions governing the conduct of military and covert operations. . . .[25]

Walsh says that "(t)he essence of the crime was not the provision of support for the contras *per se,* nor were the conspirators charged simply with conspiring to violate the Boland Amendment as such. Rather, the essence of the crime was the deceit of Congress. . . ."[26]

How did North deceive Congress according to Walsh? North found a loophole in the laws. In Walsh's "inquisition-land" view of justice, it was a criminal offense for North to use the loophole in the law rather than telling Congress about the loophole so they could plug it. North was guilty, says Walsh, of finding ways to do things that he knew Congress would make illegal if they knew about them! He was guilty of the crime of not breaking the law! (Egad!!!)

> The conspirators, aware of the statutory efforts to limit and allow Congress to monitor funding for military operations of the contras, chose to hide their activities from Congress – with the aim of ensuring that Congress would not have the opportunity to consider whether to close such a loophole.[27]

Reading Walsh's definition of conspiracy and criminal activity gives one the distinct impression that this man learned criminal law by watching Tales From the Crypt or one of Steven Spielberg's psycho-thrillers. He is a figure straight out of the medieval inquisition legends.

His principle appears to be: if Congress has not passed a law, but you think they might want to, it is illegal for you to do what appears to be legal, because they would make it illegal if they knew. In olden days, men stricken with such mental convolutions spent most of their time in dungeons breaking legs and exacting quotas of flesh.

It makes no difference to Walsh that the Boland Amendments were part of appropriations bills and had no criminal penalties attached to them. Since North tried to find ways to help the Contras without violating the Boland Amendment, the attempt not to be covered by Congress's law was itself a criminal offense. At least that is the ex cathedra verdict echoing through the corridors which exit the Independent Counsel's dimly lit dungeon.

Resisting the Coup

In constitutional contests with Congress, the President is at a distinct disadvantage. Congress has the power to pass "laws." The President can only give speeches and issue orders.

Congress can tilt in their own favor any dispute between the White House and Congress about constitutional separation of powers simply by "passing a law" designed to take some of the president's power away. Sometimes when a president signs a bill into law, such restrictions are buried obscurely beneath a mountain of words and paper on other matters.

Congress got the upper hand in the Iran/Contra matter because it could disguise its attack on the executive branch by hiding behind the mask of legitimate lawmaking. Many Americans were fooled by this ploy, believing that North was a criminal. As at other times in America's history, the President could only defend the powers of his office by standing firm, despite Congress's intrusion, for as long as possible.[28]

ELEVEN

Why Reagan Slept

Congress's Secret Coup Goes Unopposed

Ronald Reagan became president in 1980 by a landslide, but entered the Oval Office on a tightrope. He assumed an office that had recently suffered tremendous injury at the hands of Richard Nixon. Two years after Nixon resigned in disgrace, Jimmy Carter began wreaking further havoc by being weak and ineffective. Carter added insult to that injury.

Carter gutted the country's intelligence apparatus while president between 1976 and 1980. With the exception of the Camp David accords, his one sterling and praiseworthy accomplishment, he left a trail of foreign policy calamities around the world which his successor would have to try to fix.

Meanwhile he signed into law a number of post-Watergate enactments designed to regulate the executive branch. These were supposed to be cooperative measures between the White House and Congress. But a number of these laws went too far. They were premised on the notion of congressional supremacy, which is contrary to our founding constitutional principles. These laws were already on the books when Reagan became president.

By the time Reagan was elected, Congress was well on its way to establishing itself as supreme over the executive branch, rather than co-equal. The legislative assault continued during Reagan's first term. Under the rubric of "ethics laws" and other regulations put in place to correct the excesses of the Nixon presidency during Watergate, Congress was whittling away at the constitutional office of the Chief Executive. All that remained was the inevitable showdown

This was the president's predicament. Congress had redefined the presidency almost to be a sub-department of Congress. The presidency was no longer on an equal par with Congress. But the spate of problems Reagan faced everywhere on the globe required him to exercise vigorous constitutional powers. He did not have the luxury of being a truncated president.

The dominant party did not share Reagan's political views nor agree with his policies. To carry out some of his policies he would have to defy Congress openly. But even worse, to carry out some of his policies he would have to keep Congress in the dark.

These new laws, post-Watergate, required him to gain approval for certain executive decisions from the very people who had every political reason not to grant him approval. The question was whether he would submit to the unconstitutional principle of parliamentary supremacy, or whether he would conduct himself as Chief Executive rather than Congress's vassal. Reagan chose the latter.

Reagan Under Siege

Less than three months after becoming president, Reagan was shot. The bullet barely missed his heart. It did not kill him, but it ended his vigor. He was already past the age where most men retire. Just staying healthy can be a challenge when you're almost 70 years old. Now he would have to recover fully from a nearly mortal wound, a feat which would not be easy even for a much younger man. Added to that were his duties as president, one of the most demanding jobs on earth.

There were the inherited problems: communism on the march controlling one-third of the world's governments; the mideast in perpetual turmoil, interest rates at 21% – problems at home and troubles abroad.

His predecessor had blinked before the communist threat. The USSR had invaded Afghanistan. Communist insurgencies were taking over Angola, Ethiopia, Nicaragua, and were undermining various other countries.

There were problems in the Philippines, El Salvador, Grenada, and Panama. Then there was the Iran/Iraq war, Libya's daffy Quadaffi, and the burgeoning international drug cartel.

Capitol Hill was controlled by the other party. Tip O'Neill welcomed Reagan to Washington by warning him that "you're in the big leagues now." Every budget proposed to Congress by Reagan was announced "DOA," dead on arrival, by the democrat leaders.

In Reagan's first term, his administration hemorrhaged from personnel losses. The reason, his political opponents resorted to a very nasty trick – ambush prosecutions on trumped up criminal charges. Reagan's opponents used politically motivated, unremitting "attack investigations" to target key associates of the President. They brought criminal accusations against them, one after another.

His opponents tried to undermine the president's friends with character assassination and innuendo. It would take years for people like Ray Donovan to be exonerated in the court system, but in the meantime, the president's agenda had been stymied.

In this hostile environment, Reagan's priorities were to defeat communism and to dampen terrorism abroad, and to restore the economy at home. He could not let anything divert him from that focus.

Twilight of Greatness

Ronald Reagan was one of the great men of this century. He was certainly one of the best presidents of this century. Unfortunately, he was in the autumn of life when he began his second term. He underwent cancer surgery in July 1985. He was no longer the same vigorous leader as before. He was in decline.

He experienced what many men his age experience: problems with short term memory loss, an increasing need for rest, and a decreasing ability to keep up a grueling pace. Instead of studying documents himself, he often received verbal briefings on them and then initialed his approval.

Far too much of his time had to be dedicated to maintaining his popularity with the public. When his time could have been better spent studying classified documents in order to make critical decisions, he was giving speeches and attending public functions to satisfy the public's need for photo opportunities. He did not have the time nor the inclination to fight with Congress over its intrusions into the Executive Branch. His fight was with America's enemies, not with Congress.

Complicating the matter was the fact that he was at the mercy his own lawyers' views of constitutionality. They advised the president, rightly so, to try as much as possible to comply with the various laws of Congress, even when in their view the laws were overbroad, unconstitutional, or intruded into the rightful purview of the president's authority.

The "new boundaries" of his legal power were not always clear. But they were always changing, as the fickle revisions of the Boland Amendment show. This put the president in a no-win situation. On one hand, he would break his oath to the Constitution if he forfeited his policy making authority to Congress. On the other hand, it was in no one's interest for him to openly provoke a standoff with Congress over foreign policy at the time when the "evil empire" was about to crumble.

In the end, Reagan did not want a showdown with Congress given the atmosphere that prevailed. The choice was made not to fight the constitutional battle should Congress ever challenge Reagan on foreign policy. Once that choice was made, the die was cast for the scapegoating of any subordinate involved in carrying out the president's policies. Oliver North, John Poindexter, and friends drew the short straws.

TWELVE

Dissecting Iran/Contra

A Trumped Up "National Scandal"

The "Iran/Contra scandal" which erupted in Reagan's second term must be recognized for what it really was, *the culmination of a ten year effort by Congress to gain control of the executive branch.* It had taken a decade for the Congress to lay the legislative trap. Iran/Contra was Congress's attempt to spring the trap and establish, once and for all, its hegemony over the Oval Office.

Again, the key is Congress's false notion of parliamentary supremacy – that Congress has the power to dictate to the president what his foreign policy should be.

It had started with Watergate but had not ended there. Richard Nixon's abuse of the presidential office gave Congress an opportunity to begin passing laws establishing itself as supreme over the executive branch. But layer upon layer of legislation was needed, taking many years to put in place.

Congress worked particularly hard to finish that legislation during Reagan's first term. Then they baited the trap with the Boland Amendment to see if Reagan would bite. He did. Finally they had the confrontation they had been seeking. And they fully expected that Iran/Contra would finish once and for all what Watergate had begun – the subordination of the Executive Branch to the Legislative Branch.

IRAN: Part One of the "Scandal"

Keep in mind that the term "Iran/Contra" represents two *supposedly* illegal parts to the same transaction. First, for reasons I will explain below, President Reagan approved the sale of military equipment to Iran. When the secret sale became known, Congress, the major media, and later the Independent Counsel assumed that the sale was illegal. Some of Reagan's own advisors and lawyers, who had bought into the false notion of parliamentary supremacy, also thought it might be illegal. It was not.

The background is this. At about the same time that Reagan entered the hospital for cancer surgery in July 1985, Israel secretly sent its special advisor on terrorism to ask help from Reagan. The Israeli government wanted to sell arms to Iran, which was at war with Iraq.

Americans generally hated Iran. The Shah of Iran, a friend of the U.S., had fallen from power during the Carter presidency. His country was taken over by radical Shiite followers of the Ayatollah Khomeini. The American embassy in Iran was overrun, and the embassy workers and diplomats were held as hostages for 444 days. They were freed on the same day that Reagan took the oath of office as President.

Iran stood between the Soviet Union and the middle eastern oil fields which contain *one-half of the world's known oil reserves*. Iran was at war with Iraq, headed by the infamous dictator Saddam Hussein. Hussein wanted to defeat Iran in order to be the uncontested leader in the Middle East. He could then grab the middle eastern oil fields for himself. By controlling one-half of the world's oil, he would wield awesome power in the international community.

Israel had everything to lose. If either side won a clear victory, Israel would be the next target. But if Iraq won the war, leaving Iran prostrate, the Soviet Union might seize the opportunity to roll through Iran on its way to the oil fields for itself. There was a real potential for World War III in the making, or at least a future war between the U.S. and Iraq.

It was in Israel's interest and in America's interest that neither Iran nor Iraq win the war. But because Iran was losing, Israel feared further radicalization of Iran and an increase in Soviet influence.

Israel's Request

Israel sought America's help to maintain a balance of power in the region. Israel believed that moderate elements in Iran could come to power if they showed the ability to defend against Iraq and to deter Soviet influence. Israel had already identified certain "western-oriented" factions within Iran's government. By giving them aid, Israel hoped to achieve some degree of influence on the government of Iran.

Israel wanted Reagan to promise to replenish Israel's supply of U.S. made weapons if Israel went ahead with a transfer of equipment to Iran. *Oliver North objected to the plan because it could not be kept secret.*[29]

American law required Israel to notify the U.S. government if it sold U.S. made arms to a third country. With all the leaks by Congress of classified information, the plan would be compromised immediately, if for no other reason than to politically embarrass Ronald Reagan.

If such a sale became public, it would become the subject of a media feeding frenzy because of American hatred toward Iran. Disclosure would make the international situation worse.

North reminded Reagan of Attorney General William French Smith's opinion that a President could sign a covert action "finding," thereby authorizing the CIA to sell arms without going through the reporting requirements.

Such a "finding" would allow the transaction to be kept secret, protecting both Israel's and the U.S.'s national interests. Israel also believed that as a by-product, the moderate Iranians could cause the Hezbollah to release a number of American hostages being held in the Middle East.

Arms For Hostages, Anyone?

Israel went ahead with its plan. Israel sent three shipments of U.S. made arms to Iran during 1985. America sent none, but helped deliver the November 1985 shipment. President Reagan signed the "finding" on January 17, 1986. The U.S. then sent five shipments of missiles or missile parts to Iran in 1986.

But when a Lebanese newspaper learned of the shipments and then went public with the information on November 3, 1986, the plan quickly fell apart.

The U.S. news media went bonkers. America had sold arms to a blacklisted terrorist country. Suspicion mounted everywhere that Reagan had "traded arms for hostages" despite his repeated insistence that the U.S. would never negotiate with kidnappers (three hostages had been released in the meantime).

Pressure mounted on the White House to make full disclosure about the sale of arms. Reagan denied that it was an arms for hostages swap. His political enemies did their best to make sure that the sale was seen in just that light, however.

Many people still think that it was an illegal arms for hostages quid pro quo. First, it was not illegal. Second, it was not arms for hostages.

The transaction was to be between governments – the United States and moderate factions within the government of Iran. The government of Iran was not holding the hostages. The hostages were held by private groups inside Lebanon. And the sale of arms was not to the Hezbollah or to other persons who were holding the hostages.

As the enclosed copy of the January 17, 1986 presidential finding shows, the transfer was not a quid pro quo, arms for hostages swap. Release of the hostages was a hoped for by-product. And Reagan had decided to stop any future transfers of arms if no hostages were released. But Reagan did not authorize an arms-for-hostages swap regardless of any spin that others then or later have put on the transfer.

The November 1985 "HAWK" Shipment

Congress, and later the Independent Counsel, tried to convince the public that either Reagan or his staff committed crimes by assisting Israel with the November 1985 shipment of HAWK missiles to Iran. Congress and Walsh alleged that the shipment was illegal because it was not preceded by a written presidential finding. Therefore, Reagan supposedly violated the law by not informing Congress. The Justice Department issued an opinion in 1985 saying that the shipment was legal.

Walsh still claims that the shipment violated the Arms Export Control Act, without citing any reason or legal precedent. However, the shipment did not violate the Arms Export Control Act, and was authorized under the National Security Act and The Economy Act.[30] The shipment was also legal in light of the 1868 Hostage Act.[31]

Moreover, *Walsh did not prosecute a single official for violating any law regarding the November 1985 HAWK shipment*. The reason is simple: none of the laws relating to the shipment were criminal laws.[32] Research by Justice Department lawyers, with reams of legal citations in support, clearly demonstrated that *no laws were broken, no criminal statutes applied, and no penalties to punish such activities existed on the books*. Similar proof of legality was published in November 1987 as part of the Minority Report of the Select Committees investigating Iran/Contra.

In short, the sale of arms to Iran – "Iran-half" of the Iran/Contra scandal – was *not* an arms for hostage swap, was *not* a criminal act on the part of the

President, and in no way violated any law of Congress. It was falsely used by the President's political opponents merely as an opportunity to attack and disable the presidency of Ronald Reagan, to try to set the stage for an unfounded attempt at impeachment.

CONTRA: Part Two of the "Scandal"

Part two of the Iran/Contra Scandal is the purported "illegal diversion" of funds to the Nicaraguan Contras following the sale of the missiles and parts to the Iranians.

Many people still believe seven years later that Oliver North, Richard Secord, and Albert Hakim took profits from the sale of missiles, profits which should have been returned to the U.S. Treasury, and instead enriched themselves and illegally sent part of the money to the Contras.

There is only one problem with this whole scenario of dastardly criminality and conspiracy. *EVERY CHARGE THAT NORTH, SECORD, OR HAKIM ILLEGALLY DIVERTED FUNDS TO THE CONTRAS WAS EITHER DISMISSED WITH PREJUDICE BY THE COURTS OR WAS DECIDED "NOT GUILTY" BY A JURY.*

Persecution Works

Good people will find it incredible to learn that the Iran/Contra hearings in 1987 were a political ploy designed to disable the Reagan White House with dubious charges of criminality. They will find it incredible that Walsh's seven-year criminal prosecution vendetta was nothing more than a poorly founded witch hunt.

The attainting, abuse, and persecution of North worked, however. Vast numbers of people still believe he is guilty of violating all sorts of laws simply because they heard congressmen on television claiming that laws were broken. The legal basis for such claims was either extremely thin or nonexistent. Congress relied on the old Goebbels propaganda dictum that if you repeat a lie loudly enough and long enough, most people will come to believe it. So far it has worked.

But the following chapters will go right to the heart of the popular myths about North's so-called criminality. If you believe in the American Constitution, and in due process within the judicial system, those myths will be exposed. *You will see Oliver North for whom he is – a truly great and patriotic American who defended the U.S. Constitution when many people around him ducked and covered.*

A great irony in this whole fiasco is that North was right in his advice to the President. Exactly five years to the day from January 17, 1986 when Ronald Reagan signed the presidential finding on the Iran initiative, Operation Desert Storm was unleashed against Saddam Hussein of Iraq. North had warned what would happen if Iraq was not contained.

When Congress (and Walsh) chose to make the Iranian initiative a *cause célèbre*, nullifying any similar opportunity by Reagan to influence the region, they practically insured the imbalance that led to the invasion of Kuwait by Iraq and the Persian Gulf War. Hundreds of Americans and over 200,000 Iraqis died as a result . . . *not to mention many secret friends.*

THIRTEEN

True Lies

The Ethics of Secrecy and the Ten Commandments

When Congress went about to attaint Oliver North, their goal was not merely to suggest that occasionally Oliver North had lied. *Instead their goal was to perpetually brand Oliver North with the reputation of "being" a liar.* The goal was to disgrace him as a person and to ruin his standing in the community forever.

If Congress's little ruse had not been so effective, I would not have taken the time to write this book. But Congress was very effective. The shame and disgrace they heaped upon Oliver North continues to hang around his neck like a giant millstone. If there is any one single opprobrium that is now most often hurled at North, it is that *he is a liar, a perjurer, someone who cannot be trusted to tell the truth.*

After the attainting, he wrongly stands forever condemned in the eyes of many people of violating one of the ten most basic rules of decent behavior, the Ninth Commandment, which says: "THOU SHALT NOT BEAR FALSE WITNESS AGAINST THY NEIGHBOR."

Orwellian Doublespeak

George Orwell's book 1984 envisioned a Big Brother government that reversed every standard of truth. In a sense, this is what was done by the Select Committees in 1987. They spent hundreds of hours and millions of dollars to brand Oliver North as a liar, when much of the time their accusations against him were false and they knew it. His inquisitors had to practice a lie to brand him as a liar.

Our forefathers intended to guard against just this form of Congressional tyranny. That is why they placed the prohibition against bills of attainder in the United States Constitution. It was included to protect a man's reputation from being destroyed for someone else's political gain.

If John Jay Were Here

John Jay was one of the Founding Fathers. He was the first Chief Justice of the United States Supreme Court. He negotiated America's peace treaty with England at the end of the Revolutionary War. He was also the first president of the American Bible Society.

In his day, the Founders accepted as a truism the biblical statement that "A good name is rather to be chosen than great riches, and loving favor rather than silver and gold."[33] They understood that the right not to be defamed, especially by your own government, was every bit as important, if not more important, than protecting a man's property rights under the law. This was part of the reason why they outlawed bills of attainder and the kind of political trial that was used to defame Oliver North.

The Bible and Covert Operations

How many times must we hear people sarcastically remark, "Ollie North doesn't even know the Ten Commandments," or, "he claims to be a born-again Christian, but he doesn't even know that its wrong to lie"?

Assuming, for the moment, that those who say this are sincere, then it is right and proper to examine the Ten Commandments and the Bible on this subject.

First, the ninth commandment forbids "bearing false witness against your neighbor." The goal of the ninth commandment is to protect the reputation and honor of man, just as the third commandment is written to protect the honor of God. North did not bear false witness against anyone.

Second, the same prophet who delivered the Ten Commandments also authorized covert spying operations and intelligence gathering activities. Moses himself was in charge of the same kind of national security and intelligence activities as Oliver North.

Moses sent out spies on a number of occasions.[34] This activity was related to covert military operations which were being planned.[35] His spy operations did not violate the ninth commandment.

Rahab's Honorable "Diversion"

Moses had his own 'Oliver North' who was the deputy director of the Israelite's national security. That man was named Joshua. Joshua became Moses's second in command when everyone else "ran for cover" during a crucial operation.[36]

After Moses died, Joshua became commander in chief. Joshua also sent out spies to gather information for crucial covert operations that were in the works. This did not violate the ninth commandment. On one occasion, Joshua sent spies to Jericho to gather information. They stayed at the home of a woman named Rahab.

Rahab accepted the spies into her home and learned of their mission. She believed in the mission and decided to help.

The king of Jericho learned that the spies were staying at Rahab's house. *He intended to find them and kill them*. He sent an executive order to Rahab by courier, commanding her to turn over the spies.[37] Instead she hid the spies.

The king sent a security detail to her house. They demanded that she tell them the whereabouts of the spies. *She had hid them on the roof of her house inside bundled stalks of flax. She knew precisely where they were*. She also knew that the officers were about to search her house. They would find the Israelites and kill them.

Rahab lied. She told the officers that the men came to her house, but she did not know where they came from. This was the first lie. Then she said that they had left town at sundown the night before, sneaking out just as the city gate was being closed and locked. This was lie number two.

Then she said, "I do not know where they went." This was lie number three. To keep the soldiers from searching her house she said, "if you go after them quickly you will be able to overtake them." This was an intentional ploy which was *knowingly* false – lie number four.

When nightfall came, she lowered the Israelites over the city wall to safety, again, a willful deception. She had "lied" repeatedly – *to save innocent life*.

Rahab is mentioned two more times in the Bible in the New Testament, and is praised for saving the lives of the Israelites. Both references call her "*righteous*," not a liar.[38] James 2:25 is particularly important on this point of ethics, because it says that she was "considered *righteous* for what she did" in hiding the spies and sending them out in a different direction.

Ordinarily, lying is absolutely ethically forbidden. But in this biblical example, Rahab misled people who intended to use the truth in a way that would endanger the lives of innocent people. *Her diversion was not morally wrong under these facts*. The Bible declares her to be "righteous" for her courageous conduct which protected innocent life.

The Hebrew Midwives

Moses, who delivered the ten commandments, reports the story of another deliberate diversion to save innocent life. Moses speaks approvingly of the event in Exodus chapter one, in the Old Testament.

The Israelites were slaves to the Pharaohs of Egypt. Near the time of Moses's birth, one Pharaoh feared the rumors of the coming deliverer. *He ordered the death of all male babies born to the Hebrew slaves*. The order was to be carried out by the Hebrew midwives whose job it was to assist in the birth process.[39]

"But the Hebrew midwives feared God, and did not as the king commanded them, but saved the men children alive," says Exodus 1:17 (KJV).

Pharaoh called the midwives before him and demanded to know why they had not obeyed his command. *They lied*. The midwives said, "the women give birth before we can get there."[40] As a consequence, "God dealt well with the midwives," and "because they feared God" he rewarded them "by giving them families of their own."[41]

This is another example where *the government intended to use the truth to punish or kill innocent people*. In that situation, God did not require the midwives to give the deadly truth to the government. Instead he blessed them and rewarded them for keeping the truth *from* the government.

The midwives believed, rightly so, that the government would misuse the truth with the result that innocent people would lose their lives. In that situation, they had *no duty to be truthful to government officials whose misuse of the truth would cause the deaths of the innocent*.

The Lessons of the Holocaust

Fifty years ago my dad risked everything to help put an end to the Nazi regime in occupied Europe. Most of his military friends died. He endured and survived the D-Day invasion and all five major campaigns in the European theater of the war. He has a chest full of medals for his service to this country and to freedom. His stories of what he saw and learned about Nazi brutality leave one speechless.

While he was in the air over Europe, doing his part to stop the Nazis, on the ground behind enemy lines a different kind of war was waged. This was the war of the German resistance and the French resistance. It was the war of one person at a time doing what he could to be a clog in the pipes of Nazi tyranny.

One such clog in the pipes was a young girl named Corrie Ten Boom. Corrie was a Christian. She and her family hid Jews, fugitives from the Nazis who were seeking to annihilate them. At the end, Corrie herself was arrested and was imprisoned in a concentration camp where she watched her sister die. Corrie survived, however, and was able to tell her story to the world for decades.

Corrie was just one of many who took incredible risks to save innocent life. The stories number in the thousands of ordinary people who intentionally deceived the Nazis to protect the Jews, and who knowingly violated the laws which required them to hand these Jews over to certain death.

We do not hold these people up to shame and disgrace for their courageous deeds. We do not ridicule them as liars or scoundrels for misleading their government. Instead we recognize them as heroes. We honor these brave souls as the very people who had their priorities straight when the rest of the world around them had gone mad.

Their selfless actions during the holocaust bear witness to a simple moral truth: *we have a duty to speak the truth, but only to those who have a right to hear the truth, and who will not misuse the truth in a way that will cause injury or death to innocent people.*

Stated another way, we have no duty to speak the truth to anyone who intends to use the truth to kill or injure others, or whose carelessness, misuse, or negligence with the truth will lead to the injury or deaths of innocent people.

The Ethics of Secrecy and Iran/Contra

Both before and during the attainder trial of Oliver North in the summer of 1987, Congress and its lawyers tried to *paint a false picture* of Oliver North and *deceive the country* about him. On the first day of his testimony in July 1987, for example, his persecutors argued that because North was involved every day with covert operations on behalf of the United States government, this somehow proved that he was a liar. It was a false argument, based on false premises, supported by false reasons.

Prosecutor Nields, for example, accused him of embracing the communist view of government because North kept secrets from the American public – classified secrets which the law forbad him to make public. Nields had to know that his innuendo against North was factually, morally, and legally wrong.

One can only conclude that he was playing to the gallery of the television audience, hoping to trick them into accepting a false argument, namely, that since Oliver North had lied to terrorists, had lied to the enemies of the United States, and had kept secret the operational details of security missions aimed at protecting the lives and welfare of innocent people around the world, North must therefore be an inveterate liar, presumptively a criminal, and no longer worthy of the public trust. Of course, that attack on North was based on sheer sophistry.

The National Security Council

The *Government of the United States* hired Oliver North to be deputy director of political and military affairs in the National Security Council. North did not create the job. The *Government of the United States* assigned Oliver North to serve under the direction of the National Security Advisor, who answered directly to the President of the United States.

It is simply fatuous for Congress, a branch of that same government, and the body who *wrote the law* creating the office, to suggest that Oliver North was a dishonorable, untrustworthy man simply by being employed *in the job they created* of directing and carrying out anti-terrorist, anti-communist covert policies. If it was wrong or immoral for North to have a job which by its very nature required him to mislead the enemies of the United States, then it was wrong for the United States Government ever to create that job!

If there was ever any substance to Congress's self-righteous condemnations of North for being involved in covert operations, then Congress is morally obligated to put an end to ALL intelligence operations, covert operations, the CIA, the FBI, the DEA, drug stings, and counter-intelligence of all kinds. In any future war, the Congress should instruct all admirals, generals, and field grade officers never to deceive the enemy because it would be morally wrong! Of course, that argument was ludicrous in 1987 when Congress slung it all over Oliver North, and it is still ludicrous today. But the key fact is that Congress knew better. Congress knew what it was doing. *The whole attack on North was a politically motivated sham.*

Lying to Congress

Ronald Reagan was right. He was right to try to bring a balance of power to the middle east. And he was right to oppose the international spread of communism. He was right to try to stop communist subversion of fledgling democracies. And he was right to encourage freedom and the rule of law in countries around the world.

Ronald Reagan assembled a team of men who shared his same love for America, his same dedication to freedom and justice for all, and his same disdain for communism and predatory, dictatorial demagogues. The major media mocked when he called the country of Lenin and Stalin "the evil empire." They mocked his reasons for trouncing the marxist coup in Grenada. They mocked when he called the Nicaraguan Contras "the moral equivalent of America's founding fathers." Oliver North did not mock.

Ronald Reagan, as president of the United States and Chief Executive, had a sworn duty to preserve, protect, and defend the Constitution of the United States. He believed that it was his duty to be the leader of the free world. He believed that it was his duty to support democratic movements around the world. He saw himself as the heir of the Truman Doctrine and the Monroe Doctrine. Consequently, he believed that he had a moral, legal, and constitutional duty to defend democracy in Nicaragua, and to oppose the spread of marxist-leninist imperialism in the western hemisphere.

When the American Congress abandoned the Contras, Reagan saw it as his duty to keep them alive "body and soul." *To do less would be to fail* as the heir of the Truman-Eisenhower-Kennedy-Johnson-Nixon anti-communist legacy. To fail to aid the Contras – the freedom fighters – would be to aid and abet the avowed enemies of the United States.

The Constitution defines treason as "adhering to the enemies of the United States," or "giving them aid and comfort." By omitting to act, Congress was giving aid and comfort to the enemies of the United States. By refusing to help those who looked to America for inspiration and the ideals of freedom, Congress was adhering to the enemies of the United States. Reagan had no other choice. He had to oppose the policies of Congress as represented by the Boland Amendment. *To do otherwise would be to deny his oath of office.*

To Protect Innocent Life

Yes, Oliver North lied, but not to Congress. He lied to terrorists and to the enemies of the United States. He did not break the law. Like Rahab, the Hebrew midwives, and those who deceived the Nazis to save the Jews, *Oliver North tried to protect innocent life*. He tried to protect the lives of our foreign operatives in Iran. He tried to protect the lives of the Democratic Resistance in Nicaragua. He tried to protect the lives of hostages in Lebanon. And he tried to protect the lives of American students in Grenada.

His involvement in covert operations was no more immoral than that which was sanctioned by Moses or Joshua in the Old Testament. And like Rahab in the Bible, *North should be praised for trying to save lives, stop terrorism, and defeat communism*. He should not be scandalized, demonized, defamed, vilified, and pilloried for helping America's friends and opposing America's enemies.

His diversions should be seen in the same light as James 2:25. Instead of being branded as a liar and a scoundrel, this stalwart patriot should be considered "righteous." He should have a "good name" rather than be forced to wear the scarlet letter of disgrace and shame.

North has even been compared to Nazis, another Orwellian reversal of meaning. North never used the so-called Nuremberg defense. He has been wildly accused of all kinds of law breaking, even treason. But he has never once said "I was just following orders."

His Marine Oath required him to swear "I will obey the lawful orders of every officer appointed over me." He served directly under the Commander-in-Chief. Do you know what the words "Commander-in-Chief" means to a Marine? North believed he was following lawful orders, not just "following orders."

To those who object that these might have been verbal orders, rather than written orders, remember this: Marines kill people with verbal orders. You'd have to be a Marine to understand. But here, rather than following *immoral* orders to take life, as the Nazis did, North was following *lawful* orders to save life. Therein lies a whole moral universe of difference.

FOURTEEN

The Game Plan

Congress, Oliver North, and the Slam Dunk

In the chapters that follow, I will sort out for you one of the most complex legal battles ever seen in the federal courts. Before taking it apart piece by piece, you need to know the Iran/Contra master game plan from Congress's playbook.

Congress intended to slam dunk Oliver North. To squeeze him into giving up the president, Congress had devised for him the political equivalent of the "Temple of Doom" in the Indiana Jones movie. Once Ollie North entered, there was supposed to be no way of escape.

Like military battles, political and legal battles are fought according to detailed plans and strategies. If you think that Congress simply intended to swarm all over Oliver North like the Celtic hordes, think again. Congress had a definite plan. It was a foolproof plan, they thought. But Oliver North is nobody's fool. He made Congress's surefire plan misfire. No slam dunk.

Many of us were oblivious to Congress's plan in 1987. Few people understood the "game winning" play that Congress had called from the sidelines. Below is a glimpse into their playbook.

Long Range Goal – Impeach Reagan

Congress's long range goal was to *impeach Ronald Reagan* to establish once and for all that Congress, not the president, controls foreign policy. To do that they had to show that Reagan was guilty of "high crimes and misdemeanors."[42] They needed to show that he had broken two laws: (1) the Arms Export Control Act's restriction on the sale of weapons to certain foreign countries, and (2) the Boland Amendment's prohibition against giving money from the U.S. Treasury to the Contras in their contest with the Sandinistas in Nicaragua.

The success of the plan depended on whether they could convince the public that Congress *already* possessed the constitutional right and authority to define and determine foreign policy. Even though Congress had written their policy into a federal law, they had to guarantee that the courts and the American people would go along with the notion of parliamentary supremacy.

Short Range Goal Number One

Convince the American Public to Accept Parliamentary Supremacy

To be able to impeach Reagan and establish itself as supreme in the realm of foreign policy, Congress first had to make sure that the voting public agreed with them. The way to do this was to use the screaming baby routine. Congress would have to "cry foul." It would have to feign "shock" and "outrage" at the possible misdeeds of the president and the executive branch.

Next, it would need to hold public hearings. By controlling the hearings, particularly if the hearings could be carried on the major networks rather than only on the cable news services, Congress could feed its point of view practically unchallenged to the entire unsuspecting public.

By holding carefully controlled and widely televised public hearings, Congress could persuade the majority to see things Congress's way. This would minimize the chance of a public opinion backlash.

Congress needed the "momentum" to cause such hearings to come about. To generate the momentum, it fed leaks to the media, hurled accusations of criminality at the executive branch, invoked images of Watergate, and served a continuous buffet of press conferences to a media hungry for controversy to build ratings. Congress got the hearings it wanted.

Short Range Goal Number Two

Persuade the Public to Assume That Laws Were Broken

To impeach Reagan, Congress had to persuade the public that Reagan had criminally violated civil laws. I think you see the immediate dilemma they faced. The Boland Amendments were restrictions on spending bills. The Boland Amendments were not criminal laws, they were civil laws. They had no criminal penalties attached to them. To make Reagan look like a criminal, Congress had to obscure the fact that Reagan, as president, had the constitutional authority to find ways to help the Contras even if Congress disagreed.

Second, they had to persuade the public to assume that if Reagan did help the Contras, he would be violating the law in a criminal way, even though the Boland Amendments were not criminal laws. This was the trickiest part of Congress's ruse. Public hearings would allow them to make the ruse work. They succeeded.

The Arms Export Control Act was only one of the laws governing the sale of military weapons to foreign countries. As explained earlier, numerous other laws gave Reagan the authority to undertake the Iranian initiative. The hearings would allow Congress to divert attention away from those laws so that they could make Reagan look like a criminal. This ploy was also reasonably successful.

Short Range Goal Number Three

Turn Reagan's Men Against Each Other

Congress had learned from Watergate how difficult it could be to get evidence of wrongdoing by going after the President directly. A president could invoke "presidential privilege" over certain documents and memos, thereby stiff arming Congress.

Even worse, Reagan was popular. People might get mad if Congress went after "Ron" directly. Congress would have to get to Ron through Ron's men.

Congress already had its villain in Oliver North. The NSC document revealing the transfer of Iranian funds to the Contras had been found by Attorney General Meese in North's office. Meese, in compliance with the law, was the one who had started the inquiry in the first place. The difference was that Meese wanted to learn if any laws had been broken. Congress assumed that they were broken. That had been their plan all along.

Shultz, at the State Department, and Weinberger, at the Defense Department, had always disagreed with the Iran initiative. Further, Shultz was jealous that the NSC was handling sensitive foreign negotiations rather than his people at the State Department. He felt slighted by the President for allowing a Marine to hold talks that State Department diplomats should be conducting. Shultz was all too willing to side with those who were bringing pressure to bear on the President's men.

Shultz and Weinberger had to tell what they knew or find themselves in contempt of Congress. When they told what they knew, the trail led to Oliver North and the NSC.

By rounding up all the president's men and forcing them to testify separately under oath, Congress expected that the pressure would make them turn against each other to escape criminal conspiracy charges. Congress identified more than fifty people involved or knowledgeable of the various operations.

Congress wanted Reagan and believed that someone would incriminate him. As Congress plowed its way through the list of witnesses, hanging the threat of prison over their heads, the noose became tighter and tighter around Oliver North's neck.

It finally came down to four people who should know: William Casey, who was already dead, Robert McFarlane, John Poindexter, and Oliver North.

Short Range Goal Number Four
Get McFarlane, North, or Poindexter To Blame Reagan

McFarlane testified before Oliver North did. But McFarlane did not incriminate Reagan. So in July 1987, North was placed in the dock for grilling. To Congress's surprise he refused to incriminate Reagan either.

North did defend himself, however. He testified that the orders came from above. McFarlane denied that they came from him. This put Poindexter in the hot seat.

Congress called Poindexter to testify. Surely he would give them Reagan to save himself. Poindexter fell on his own sword. He told Congress that Reagan did not know, and that he, Poindexter, had given the orders to North. North thought they had come from the President, when they had come from Poindexter.

Congress had just swung for strike three. They did not have Reagan. There would not be a full blown impeachment of the president of the United States. They would not attain their long range goal of supremacy over the executive branch, at least not completely, and not yet.

Congressional Medal Of *Dis*honor

Squeeze Play to Make the Marine Cry Uncle

When North was hauled before Congress in July 1987, this was the implied threat. *'We have everything we need to pin this thing on you. Give us Ronald Reagan, or we will ruin you for life and make sure that you go to jail.'*

They were giving North the Hobson's Choice.[43] To betray his Commander in Chief would be to humiliate himself as a Marine. This was totally unthinkable. It would be worse than death itself. But not to betray the president meant that North would falsely be *branded as a criminal, a scoundrel, a liar, the scum of the earth, a renegade, a fanatic, and an uncontrollable self-willed zealot.* His reputation would be forever ruined. His future would be ruined. He would go down in history as a man despised and disgraced. His name would live in infamy.

Marines live by the motto 'Death Before Dishonor.' To North, this was worse than death. He found himself forced to make an utterly reprehensible choice between two equally despicable alternatives, dishonor or dishonor.

- Bill of Attainder

Part one of the squeeze play, as we have already said, was the attainting of North. If North did not hand over the president he would be castigated and condemned forever by Congress.

Congress could exonerate North if he gave up the president. If he did not, they would finish what they had begun, namely, destroying his reputation in the eyes of the American public.

Congress was not worried that bills of attainder are unconstitutional. Most Americans have forgotten this part of the Constitution anyway. Plus, Congress had already put substitute methods in place so that they could ruin a man's reputation without appearing to violate the Constitution.

- The Independent Counsel Law.

Congress created a method of avoiding blatant violations of the bill of attainder clause by putting the Independent Counsel law (sometimes called the Special Prosecutor law) on the books. They commissioned the special prosecutor to "investigate" and "publish his conclusions." Since *he* publishes the conclusions instead of Congress, there appears to be no violation.

Even though Congress does not publish the bill of attainder directly, the bill nevertheless is *published by someone to whom Congress has delegated the power.*

Moreover, the independent counsel law itself violates the bill of attainder clause of the Constitution because of the section which allows the IC to publish accusations of guilt and label a man as a criminal in disregard of the constitutional guarantees of judicial due process. Walsh submitted his final conclusions of North's criminality on August 4, 1993.

Remember, however, that the Supreme Court has ruled that the bill of attainder clause can be violated *even if Congress does not publish the bill.*[44] Otherwise, Congress could go through all the motions of ruining someone with a political trial (which they did with the Iran/Contra hearings) but avoid violating the constitution simply by not publishing their conclusions.

According to the Supreme Court, if Congress goes through the motions of attainting someone with a political trial, this violates the Constitution even if they do not at the end publish the bill. (Congress published its own "report" in November 1987. Walsh published his final report in 1993. Either way, the bill was published, in violation of the Constitution.)

- The Fifth Amendment

The Constitution's Fifth Amendment says that a man cannot be forced to testify against himself. North *was* forced to testify against himself, because he was "granted immunity."

- Forced Testimony

Congress passed a law to force people to testify. In theory, they can order you to testify, *despite* the Fifth Amendment, since they promise to "grant you immunity from prosecution," meaning that nothing you say can be used against you in a court of law.

However, in 1987 the promise of immunity was a hoax and Congress knew it. *Congress knew* that a number of federal appeals courts and a number of lower federal district courts had gutted the supposed "protections" of the use immunity statute *by carving out exceptions* to the rule.

- Empty Promises.

Congress knew that North's testimony could be used against him even though they had promised that it would not be. North knew this also. So did North's lawyer, Brendon Sullivan. North knew that the so-called protection was phony, at least in the eyes of Congress and in the eyes of the special prosecutor, Lawrence Walsh.

Congress had every reason to believe that North's testimony would be used to gain an indictment of him by the Grand Jury. Congress had every reason to believe that the "immunized testimony" would later be used to convict him of crimes in a court of law. Guaranteeing that North would be indicted and later judged a felon because of his own forced testimony was *part of Congress's plan* from the very beginning.

- Congress Knew that North Knew

Congress granted North immunity, not because they believed it would shield him from being found guilty in a court of law, but because they knew that North knew the "protection" was an illusion. This would create even more psychological pressure on him. They wanted to create in him a *feeling of helplessness*, that there would be no way out for him unless he betrayed Reagan. This was another ploy to try to force him to give them Ronald Reagan.

Since North knew that the "protection" was phony, every word of testimony was one more nail in his legal coffin unless he betrayed Reagan. Every time he opened his mouth before the Select Committee he was giving them more rope with which the Special

Prosecutor would hang him in the criminal trial that was to follow. The fix was in from the beginning.

- Connect the Dots

All Congress needed to do was to look for minor differences between everyone's version of who said what to whom and when. Either someone would break under the pressure and lie about others to save himself, or Congress could infer guilty conduct by the different pieces of testimony. Plus, they had hundreds of thousands of documents, and boxes of inter-agency and interoffice data at their disposal.

- Catch-22

Congress put Oliver North in the perfect Catch-22. He could stand firm and make himself the goat. Or he could cave and give them the President. He refused to give them the President.

When he would not bend or break, the Committees unleashed all their fury against him to strip him of any honor or any shred of respectability. Then they handed him over to the Lawrence Walsh, the Grand Inquisitor, to undergo a trial which was fixed from the beginning.

Oliver North was finished in the eyes of many in the community. All that remained for him was to await a guilty verdict which had already been guaranteed by Congress's shrewd duplicity.

The sad part of this is that Reagan may have been able to stop the entire process by going head to head with Congress over the issue of separation of powers. Neither the Iran initiative nor the effort to help the

Contras was illegal. That Reagan chose not to do so is understandable for the reasons given earlier.

- The Watergate Pox

There is a separate reason why Reagan may have chosen not to fight Congress, however. Congress could barely wait to saddle Reagan with the Watergate comparison. Had Reagan dug in his heels, this would have played right into the hands of Congress. If he claimed executive privilege, his detractors would have immediately compared him to Richard Nixon.

In addition, a number of Supreme Court opinions had upheld various Watergate-style process laws, making it more difficult for the President to confront Congress.

Then there is the dreaded word "*coverup*" that is the political kiss of death to a president after Watergate, even Teflon Ron. The media would have made the connection instantly. Reagan could not in any way give the impression that he was assisting a coverup.

To avoid the Watergate curse, Reagan *chose to let Congress have its way* and chose to provide everything the special prosecutor needed to ruin the President's men. There was no cavalry charge by Reagan to rescue his friends. This was truly Death Valley Days. In light of the damage that was wrongly done not only to Oliver North but to so many other good men, Reagan's decision on how to deal with the Iran/Contra matter is one of the more disappointing decisions of his career.

FIFTEEN

The Six-Million Dollar Man

The Price of Justice for Oliver North

After Congress had completed its dirty work of attainting Oliver North, they turned loose their attack dogs from the special prosecutor's office.

The grand inquisitor, Lawrence Walsh, spearheaded the government's campaign to destroy Oliver North in the courts. It cost Ollie six million dollars to see the battle through to the end, finally to be exonerated at the federal appeals level.

Walsh had the entire budget of the U.S. Government at his disposal. Money was no object. Estimates are that he spent directly about $40 million dollars investigating and carrying out the Iran/Contra prosecutions.

When costs to the other departments and agencies of the government are taken into account (complying with his subpoenas and outrageous demands for documents was very expensive), the final tally is somewhere in the neighborhood of $100 million.[45]

Walsh was accountable to no one. He wasted seven years and tens of millions of dollars on his *jihad,* despite being chided – rebuked really – by the Appeals Court for his misconduct.[46] One might indeed wonder why he squandered tens of millions of tax dollars just to punish Oliver North for getting a security fence.

Terminate With Prejudice

Lawrence Walsh had an incredible opportunity. He could be remembered as ***the lawyer*** who hung a president's scalp on his belt. This is a powerful temptation to a prosecutor. It was a powerful incentive for Walsh to do whatever it took to "expose" Reagan as the godfather of a scandalous criminal conspiracy – a conspiracy that existed only in Walsh's mind and imagination, because the initiatives were never illegal in the first place.

More than anything, he wanted to get Reagan, to get the hard evidence that Reagan had known and approved the Iran/Contra operation. To do that, he followed a "scorched-earth" policy of harassing, intimidating, persecuting, and prosecuting as criminals dozens of people who had been directly or indirectly in contact with the Iran/Contra matter.

He had the power to manipulate the grand jury system. He had almost unlimited power to investigate the Executive Branch and to demand that it divulge every tiny shred of information, down to the last needle in the last haystack. He had the power to manipulate the trial system, and did so.

And he used every weapon in his arsenal to judicially rape North, Poindexter, and thirteen other defendants to make them testify that the President, his top advisors, and Cabinet officers were the ones who had called all the shots in Iran/Contra. Walsh pursued them with rabid tenacity.

By crushing the bones of North and Poindexter under the heavy wheels of his judicial steamroller, Walsh could pave his way right up to the Oval Office. There he would offer the president a ride, straight down the road to impeachment and then to prison.

Yes, he was willing to break the bank to have the mounted head of Ronald Reagan hanging on the wall of his trophy room. But again, Walsh failed to understand just who it was he was up against on this little safari. You don't try to trophy hunt a Marine.

"Walshington, D.C."

Nothing like this has been seen here since the British sacked and burned Washington in the War of 1812. Congress gave Lawrence Walsh free rein to plunder and pillage practically every file cabinet and storage bin in the city.

In January 1987, within weeks of being appointed, Walsh directed his teams to begin interviewing dozens of witnesses and reviewing hundreds of thousands of documents.[47] A Grand Jury was empaneled to review the documents. It sat for twenty four months, ending its review on January 27, 1989.[48]

In February the nerve center of the inquisition was moved to downtown Washington, D.C., to a building with one of the most expensive floor space rentals in the city. Special storage areas were constructed there to house the hundreds of boxes of classified documents that were brought to Walsh from all over the city.

Walsh summoned the government to disgorge all "handwritten and typed notes, computer records and disks, diaries, appointment calendars and schedules, tapes and films, phone logs, correspondence, memos, messages, reports, studies, minutes, transcripts, work papers, agendas, announcements, computer notes and messages, telegrams, teletypes, bank records and other records," anything having remotely to do with Iran/Contra.[49]

Walsh demanded that the White House surrender any information or materials regarding "(1) the sale or shipment of arms to Iran, and contacts with nine listed Iranians; (2) the sale or shipment of arms to Iran, using but not limited to 26 intermediaries; (3) the diversion of proceeds" to the Contras involving "but not limited to 25 listed individuals and business concerns; (4) the provision of support to the . . . contras, including possible contacts with 71 listed individuals and organizations; (5) meetings of 17 listed Administration working groups; (6) the calendars, schedules, phone logs and travel records of 34 listed White House and other officials; (7) computer messages generated or received by 35 White House staff members" and an almost infinite number of other items.[50]

Walsh's investigation settled on Washington like a plague of locusts. By the end of April 1987, only four months into the process, and before the televised hearings began, Walsh had already interviewed over 800 "witnesses" and had collected hundreds of boxes of documents from the White House and various agencies.[51] This was taking place at the same time that

Congress itself was receiving massive amounts of secret and classified information in pursuit of its own investigation prior to the hearings.

Many of the communications between North and others had taken place through the computer message system at the White House and the Executive Office building. This system was supposed to be secure. Once a classified message was sent to another through the system, the sender could push the "delete" button and supposedly erase any trace of the message.

Experts working for the Tower Commission's investigation in December 1986 found a way to revive all the deleted messages. Every letter, memo, note, and comment that was ever sent by North or Poindexter over the system was retrieved and handed over to the Special Prosecutor. There were no secrets left about Iran/Contra once that happened.

Rampaging Probe

When the trial judge got into the act, he issued order after order at the Prosecutor's request to scour, search, and comb practically every inch of government property for information. "In July 1988 alone, the government produced 350,000 pages of documents in response to the court's expanded discovery order."[52]

So many classified documents were required to be handed over, that a special Interagency Review Group was created to read each document line by line to determine what parts could be made public at trial and what must be marked through in black to keep as a government secret.

At North's trial, hundreds of exhibits were admitted into evidence, many which had previously been top secret and higher. These covered his activities in the Middle East, Europe, Africa, Central America, South America, and Asia[53] The Prosecutor also demanded North's personal notebooks, which were his own property and not the government's. He was forced to surrender 2,617 pages of notes from January 1984 to November 1986, despite the Fifth Amendment guarantee not to be forced to incriminate himself.

Double Cross and Double Standard

When preparations were underway for the trial, the lower judge ruled repeatedly in favor of the prosecutor. North's lawyers had to file over 100 defense motions to protect North from being abused by an already rigged outcome. Most of those motions were denied.

The search by the prosecutor had brought in 900,000 classified documents which would be used in evidence against North. The judge would only allow North to flip through the documents *in camera*, that is, in private in the judge's chambers.[54] There was no way he could review, arrange, and organize his defense from those documents under those conditions.

After much wrangling, the prosecutor told the judge that about 50,000 pages of core documents were relevant to the prosecution. North was allowed to view these documents *in camera*.[55] North was required to tell the Prosecutor which documents North intended to use for his defense, and the purpose for which he would use them. In effect, the judge required North to tell the prosecutor his entire defense strategy, meaning that North was being required to lay out the case against himself – to do the prosecutor's job for him.[56]

Perverse Obsession

The Special Prosecutor's fixation on acquiring documents did not abate with the North trial. By his own admission, the Independent Counsel "was able to recover hundreds of thousands of relevant materials."[57] These were produced for five separate grand juries. The first, as mentioned above, sat for two years from January 1987 until January 1989.

The second was convened on May 15, 1990 and sat for two years until May 15, 1992. The third sat in the Eastern District of Virginia, the fourth in Baltimore, Maryland, and the fifth in Washington, D.C. Hundreds of boxes and hundreds of thousands of pages of classified data were gathered this way.

In January 1990, the Special Prosecutor sought to obtain millions of documents seized by the United States after invading Panama and arresting Gen. Manuel Noriega.[58] He even sent three investigators to Panama to review documents there which might tell him something about North's contacts with Noriega.

On one occasion, Walsh had subpoenas prepared for former officials of the Government of Israel and had them put on a "watch list." If they entered the United States they would be served with subpoenas.

When the former Israeli Director-General of Foreign Affairs, the most senior position in the Israel's foreign ministry, visited the U.S., he answered a knock at his hotel room door and was handed a subpoena by two federal agents. It ordered him to appear before a

Grand Jury within two days. This man was Israel's spy chief. His Prime Minister was not a happy camper.

The Government of Israel was forced to go to court in the United States to protest Walsh's conduct and contest the subpoena. This international incident, which would not have been tolerated had another country acted this way toward a United States ambassador, was merely the final insult to Israel by the Special Prosecutor. For more than a year, Walsh had refused to enter into an agreement with Israel or respect its sovereign rights under international law.[59]

After this incident, Walsh signed an agreement with the government of Israel and was given access to an enormous amount of classified Israeli government information dealing with the Iran initiative. But there was nothing to find.

Coming Away Empty Handed

After seven years of scouring, rummaging, ransacking, searching, groping, prying, probing, using the drift net, and dissecting the U.S.'s top secrets, the Grand Inquisitor could not get North *or* Reagan.

Colonel North was acquitted by the trial jury on all but three charges. Then the appeals court held that he was wrongly convicted on those three charges and overturned the verdicts. Walsh grudgingly admitted that he "found no credible evidence that President Reagan had violated any criminal statute."[60] So much for the trophy mount. And as for North, Walsh concluded that he and Poindexter were the "scapegoats whose sacrifice would protect the Reagan Administration in its final two years."[61] Go figure.

SIXTEEN

The Big Lie

Puncturing the Myths About Oliver North's "Guilt"

This book seeks to undo the wrongful attainting of Oliver North. The goal is not to explain away any real guilt, but to show how he was falsely accused and falsely condemned *from the beginning*. Admittedly this is only a small first step in light of the millions spent to ruin him. But justice and honor require it. The Big Lie *about* Oliver North has prevailed far too long.

After five years of being crushed, first by Congress and then by implacable persecutors from the IC's office, Oliver North was acquitted and exonerated by the Appeals Court of the United States.

Despite that victory, much deserved and long overdue, *his reputation is still ruined* in the eyes of very many Americans. He has been permanently vilified – unconstitutionally *attainted* – a punishment for him which was one of Congress's major goals.

He is seen as a "convicted felon," a criminal who was "let off on a technicality." Thus his victory in the federal appeals court is hollow. He still wears a badge of infamy. He has been branded a pariah.

Untangling the Knot

The various rulings, orders, motions, and court opinions from North's legal war with Walsh cover hundreds of pages in the law books where they are reported. But the essence of them is simple and easy to understand. In the pages that follow, I will explain Walsh's legal attack on North piece by piece, and how the case against him fell apart, and finally failed entirely.

I will also speak directly to the prevailing myths about Colonel North's alleged "guilt." If you put yourself in his shoes as you read these chapters, you will see why the epithets and denigrations of his character are totally undeserved.

• He was indicted by a Grand Jury, yes. But *the indictments were obtained illegally*, because the Grand Jury was manipulated by the prosecutor.

• He was indicted on 16 counts. But *four* of those counts *had to be dropped* – at the prosecutor's request – because the prosecutor learned that the charges were unconstitutional or unfactual, and could never be sustained in a court of law. Those four counts represented the main thrust of Walsh's case against North.

• He was tried on 12 counts, and convicted initially on three. The jury found him not guilty as to *every Iran/Contra related "crime" publicly charged to him by the congressional committees in the televised hearings!*

• When the appeals court examined the three convictions, it ***vacated all three, reversed one outright,*** and rebuked the trial judge and the special prosecutor for violating the Constitution by failing to give North a fair trial or due process.

• Some of the judge's instructions to the jury had been *wrong*. Therefore the jury was obligated to bring in a guilty verdict on at least one of the three convictions when they should not have. And the jury was wrongly influenced toward a guilty verdict on another.

• Two of the three guilty verdicts had been *improperly obtained*.

• All that was left was North's "crime" of accepting a security fence to protect his family from published threats of assassination by the Abu Nidal terrorist organization. They were furious with North for thwarting their terrorist activities, for freeing hostages, and for doing such things as stopping the Achille Lauro hijacking (which happened shortly afterward). North was a nightmare to America's terrorist enemies. He did this for you, pilgrim.

• If it were not for politics, alluded appeals judge Silberman, "it is unlikely, perhaps inconceivable, that such a person would actually have been prosecuted for accepting a security fence soon after his life had been publicly threatened by a Palestinian terrorist group."[62]

• Judge Silberman viewed the prosecutor's comments to the jury about the security fence to be so outrageous (violating a written agreement on the rules of engagement in court), and so *intentionally* improper, that he reprimanded the lawyer for prosecutorial misconduct.[63] Had this been a U.S. Attorney rather than a special prosecutor, he would likely have recommended disciplinary action against the lawyer.[64]

• Moreover, the terrorist threats against North were completely unrelated to Iran/Contra. They were made because of his effective anti-terrorist measures on behalf of the President of the United States. But his own government, the Congress, and the Department of Defense refused to protect North and his family! He had become too controversial. Apparently, some people would rather have seen him dead. I wonder why.

• The law dictates that he had a right to protect himself, to protect his wife, and to protect his children. The *right to self-defense* is as old as the common law and is backed by constitutional guarantees.

• To call the security fence "a gratuity" as if it were a bribe for political favors, which is precisely how Congress and the special prosecutor characterized it, is a malevolent and despicable twisting of the truth. Thus the guilty verdict, improperly obtained, was a travesty. To make Colonel North out to be a criminal for trying to save lives is unAmerican and unconscionable. As always, he was doing his duty.

If you have any doubts, go to Quantico. Strike up a conversation with a Marine, any Marine. See what happens when you tell him that it is okay for terrorists to kill his little girl who is only eleven years old. Tell him he ought to go to jail if he does something to stop it. Argue your point with vigor. Talk down to him. And take a neck brace with you. You may need it for the ride home.

SEVENTEEN

The Indictments and Verdicts

The Truth Behind the Layers of Muck

The accusers of Oliver North try to have it both ways. First they say that he would have been easily convicted *on all charges* if only his immunized testimony to Congress could have been used in court. But then they insist that his guilty verdicts were overturned *because* his immunized testimony was used in court. They cannot have it both ways. Which is it?

They continue to insist that he "got off on a technicality" when he did not. They persist in calling him a "convicted felon" even though the verdicts were overturned. And they remain convinced that he lied to Congress when he did not.

Is it true that "the only reason he was *not* convicted on all the charges was because of the grant of immunity"? Would he "most certainly have been convicted on *all* counts" if his testimony before Congress had been allowed in court?

Ask yourself . . . if his testimony was not used in court, how did he "get off on the technicality" that his testimony was used? Inquiring minds want to know.

What Really Happened

North's testimony before Congress was used at the trial, as I shall show.[65] But even then the jury found him *Not Guilty* of the principal charges against him. The jury found him

- Not Guilty of obstruction of Congress in September and October of 1985. (Count One).
- Not Guilty of false statements to Congress in a September 5, 1985 letter. (Count Two).
- Not Guilty of false statements to Congress in a September 12, 1985 letter. (Count 3).
- Not Guilty of false statements to Congress in an October 7, 1985 letter. (Count 4).
- Not Guilty of obstruction of Congress in August 1986. (Count 5).
- Not Guilty of obstruction of Congress in November 1986. (Count 6).
- Not Guilty of obstructing a Presidential inquiry in November 1986. (Count 7).
- Not Guilty of lying to the Attorney General during his investigation on November 23, 1986. (Count 8).
- Not Guilty of illegally converting traveler's checks to his own use. (Count 11).
- Not Guilty of a conspiracy with others to defraud the United States Treasury and the IRS. (Count 12).

In other words, the jury found him NOT GUILTY of ALL the key charges which gave rise to the televised hearings in the first place. The jury did that; not the Appeals Court! He was not let off on a technicality.

Notice what the indictments do not allege. Many people wrongly believe that Oliver North was accused of lying under oath to a committee of Congress. He never did so, and was never charged with having done so! He was never charged with personally making false statements before any congressional committee or any other legislative group. He was accused and acquitted of making misleading statements in letters and memoranda prepared at the direction of Robert McFarlane. He did not lie to Congress.

It may be hard for some to grasp the fact that the jury had all the information it needed to convict Oliver North on all counts *if he was indeed guilty*.

The trial lasted for twelve weeks.[66] The Prosecutor had at his disposal the mountain of classified evidence which I explained to you in chapter fifteen. He had over 5,000 computer E-mail messages from John Poindexter alone.

Walsh had reams of documentation of the Iran arms deal from every branch of the U.S. government and also from the Israeli government. He had an equally massive amount of data about the Nicaraguan operation.

The prosecutor relied on two basic sources of information. He had the combined take from the unprecedented plundering of the federal government's files, and he had the testimony of 31 prosecution witnesses who were immersed in Oliver North's testimony.[67]

Marines are familiar with this kind of ambush technique. First, you set up a field of fire, a "kill zone," with two rifle squads situated across from each other at oblique angles. Next, you lure the enemy into the field of fire. By the time he realizes he is helplessly trapped it is too late. He is caught in the crossfire and cannot retreat. If he tries to flee, he escapes into trip wires, booby traps, and land mines.

The prosecutor's trial strategy was similar. He had set up his field of fire, his prosecutorial "kill zone," with the two sources of information. North was in the crossfire, a barrage of evidence coming from both sides. Colonel North was surrounded with judicial tripwires, booby traps and landmines, having no way to escape. Meanwhile the crosshairs of the prosecutor's sniper scope were coolly aligned over North's heart.

The Key Legal Issue

That Oliver North was involved in the Iran arms sale was never in question. That he was involved in funding the Contras was never in question. What he said or did with respect to the Attorney General's investigation or Congress's investigation was never in question. The documentation was overwhelming. The basic facts of Iran/Contra were never in dispute at the trial.

The question was one of illegality. Was North's activity illegal? And did he violate the following laws either by lying to Congress or otherwise: 18 US Code § 1505 and 2; § 1001 and 2; § 2071(b) and 2; § 201(g), 201(c)(1)(b) and 2; § 654 and 371. The jury cleared him of every charge of false statements to Congress! He did not violate any law of the United States on that point!

The Three "Convictions"

- The jury delivered three guilty verdicts involving Count 6, Count 9, and Count 10.
- The Appeals Court struck down the conviction for Count 9 because the trial judge gave the jury the wrong instructions.

Count Nine Conviction Reversed

Not a Technicality

Count Nine accused Colonel North of violating 18 U.S.C. § 2071 by illegally "destroying altering, or removing official NSC documents" in defiance of an NSC regulation. The trial judge instructed the jury to ignore all evidence of authorization in deciding whether North had a criminal intent to break the law. The jury came back with a guilty verdict.

The Appeals Court overturned that verdict, pointing out that if North was authorized, this would negate any criminal intent, and therefore the jury should have been allowed to consider such authorization.[68]

The law required North to act with the knowledge of unlawfulness. Section 2071 is a very strict law requiring a high degree of criminal intent. The Appeals Court noted that belief that one's actions are authorized by one's superiors "can affect a defendant's *belief* that his conduct was lawful — particularly when we are dealing in an areas of international security concerns, and when the authorization is thought to come from the President himself."[69]

Walsh had linked the criminal standards of Section 2071 to an internal regulation at the White House requiring that in the ordinary course of events, certain documents should be preserved rather than destroyed.

The Appeals Court pointed out that since it was the President's own regulation, he could change it or override it if he so chose. If North believed that he was operating at the President's direction, whether specific or implied (e.g., through North's superiors), he could reasonably believe that the President's direction overrode the regulation. Consequently, there would be no violation of Section 2071.[70] The Court said:

> We surely could not hold that it is *unreasonable as a matter of law* to believe that one's superiors in the NSC, including the National Security Advisor himself, could authorize the destruction of internal NSC documents, especially when only an NSC regulation prohibits their destruction in the first place. This last point is critical because it makes it all the more plausible that the jury would credit North's claim that he did not think he was acting unlawfully. Thus, the jury should have been able to consider the evidence of authorization in the record that was excluded by the District Court's instructions even if it had been determining whether North reasonably believed his conduct was not unlawful.[71]

The Appeals Court thought it important that "McFarlane sent North a note on November 8, 1986 stating that he hoped 'someone was purging the NSA traffic files on [a matter relating to the Iranian arms shipment].'"[72]

The key was whether North believed his actions were legal. The Appeals Court said: "If he did so believe, then his course was not illegal or even dubious. The District Court's instruction in effect makes violation of the regulation a *per se* violation of the statute without regard to the defendant's belief that his authorization from the highest echelons of the executive branch could trump a regulation about document control."[73] "[A]uthorization being the core defense — North's conviction on Count 9 must be reversed."[74]

Walsh and North's detractors would have you believe that this count was reversed on a technicality, namely, the use of North's immunized testimony at trial. Even though a violation of the Fifth Amendment is hardly a "technicality," *it does not even apply here*.

The reversal of Count 9 was substantive. The trial judge required the jury to find North guilty even if he could prove to them that the law was not broken. So they did. And that is why the Appeals Court reversed the conviction. The jury had been forced by the judge to reach the wrong result under the law.

Judge Silberman, in his concurring opinion, makes the point even more bluntly.

> The crucial point here is that, as we have recognized, . . . destroying these documents is not a criminal act in and of itself unless it is done with subjective knowledge of unlawfulness. Indeed, we reverse the conviction on Count 9

> precisely because we conclude that the jury had been improperly instructed on the issue of North's intent, therefore making illegitimate the jury's conviction on that count. . . . Destroying documents (whether or not in violation of regulations) is not a crime. Government officials, particularly those who deal with security matters, often shred documents as a matter of course — to do otherwise might create serious dangers or, in some circumstances, violate the law. Therefore, when the jury decides, as it must, whether the endeavor was undertaken corruptly, it could not conclude that "destroying documents," without regard to purpose, is a corrupt means of obstructing the committee....
>
> North claimed that he destroyed and altered these documents — pursuant to the direct instructions of Casey, Poindexter, McFarlane, and the indirect instructions of President Reagan — in order to protect sensitive covert operations involving Iran and the Contras.[75]

So Walsh and Congress had it wrong all along (as they already knew). It is not a crime to destroy documents if it is part of one's job or if one has the authority to do so. In some instances it is a crime not to destroy documents. There are hundreds of shredding machines slicing away and hundreds of burn bags being incinerated all over Washington, D.C., and throughout the U.S. Government even as you read this sentence. That is why the conviction on Count 9 was reversed.

EIGHTEEN

Convicted on a Technicality
Count 6: Aiding and Abetting

So far we have seen that the jury acquitted North on ***ten of the twelve*** principal charges. It entered guilty verdicts on Counts 9 and 10. The Appeals Court ***reversed*** Count 9. This left one principal charge, Count 10 – the security fence.

But because the trial judge gave the jury the wrong verdict forms and then gave the jury more wrong instructions, the jury handed down a separate guilty verdict of "aiding and abetting" for Count 6.

For those who believe that North "got off on a technicality" at the Appeals Court level, the guilty verdict on Count 6 for aiding and abetting obstruction is a good example of how he was made a felon on a "technicality." Drum roll please. . . .

The Special Verdict Forms

The trial judge allowed the jury to use the wrong verdict forms for Counts 6 and 9 at the end of North's trial.[76] The jury should have been given what are known as "general verdict" forms.

A *general verdict* form gives the jury one shot at finding the defendant guilty or not guilty of each count. The jury enters a check mark on the line beside the words "not guilty" or on the line beside the words "guilty." There should be one verdict for each Count.

A *special verdict* form, which should not have been used for this kind of trial, gives the jury two shots at finding the defendant guilty on each count. A defendant can be found ***not guilty*** of the primary charge, but still be found "guilty" of aiding and abetting others who may have broken the law.

When the jury enters a checkmark on the line beside the first "not guilty," it may still enter a checkmark on the line beside "guilty" beneath the words "aiding and abetting."

This means that the jury had at least four chances of convicting North of two crimes.[77] So it found him "Not Guilty" at least eleven times on twelve counts.

This is significant because North's testimony before Congress was used at the trial. I will explain this more fully later. North's critics are wrong to say that he most certainly would have been found guilty on all points had his immunized testimony been used against him.

The fact of the matter is that he was forced to *testify against himself* because his congressional testimony was used against him. But the jury found him "Not Guilty" on most of the principal charges nevertheless. [Remember, the only reason he was going through all this was because Congress had presumed to made it "illegal" for the Executive Branch not to answer politically motivated inquiries by Congress.]

The "President Trap"

I have already explained that Congress had tried to take presidential power away under the *pretext* of passing valid laws. President Reagan was at a disadvantage in this fight because Congress could simply point to its own laws, though of dubious constitutionality, and accuse the President of becoming a criminal.

The President cannot write a law protecting his power if Congress intrudes, he can only object to Congress's intrusion and try to stand his ground. If the public has bought into the idea of parliamentary supremacy, they will assume that Congress's laws are valid and that therefore Congress's intrusion into the executive branch is valid. Indeed, they will be unaware that Congress *is* intruding. If the President resists Congress, he becomes a criminal by definition.

In this kind of unfair fight, *the President automatically loses* in the eyes of the public. And since his actual power to lead and to command is political only – because his power rests solely on popular support – he is completely dependent on whether he is viewed favorably or unfavorably by the majority. The right kind of bad press will destroy his presidency. That's our system.

Casey, McFarlane, and Poindexter understood this fact clearly. Although the *Iran initiative* was legal, Congress had the ability to make it *appear to be* illegal and use it as a political battering ram to bring down the President.

Although the *Nicaraguan initiative* was legal, Congress had the ability to make it *appear to be* illegal and use it as a political battering ram to bring down the President. They had already indicated their intention to do so. *They aimed to turn a dispute over foreign policy into a White House criminal conspiracy.* Now was the time.

The President was still recovering from cancer surgery. He was not at one hundred percent. He probably was not even at seventy percent. Congress ordered Casey and Poindexter to appear on November 21, 1986 before three congressional committees to testify about the U.S. role in the November 1985 shipment of Israeli missiles to Iran. The 'prey' was wounded and the vultures were circling overhead.

Casey, it appears, decided to protect the president (possibly at Reagan's specific direction). He could not tell Attorney General Ed Meese or ask Meese's opinion, because Congress had hog tied the attorney general with a whole range of other intrusive and possibly unconstitutional laws. Meese was trumped.

Congress's "trap" for the president was working beautifully. Casey was sure that Congress would politically misuse the fact that the Iran initiative had been publicly exposed. He instructed McFarlane, Poindexter, and North to hide the details of the NSC's and the President's involvement in the November 1985 shipment.

The False Chronology

Oliver North was ordered to redraft the chronology of the 1985 Iran initiative. [Remember, the Iran initiative was legal, but Congress intended to make it appear to be illegal.] Casey wanted to hide the truth from Congress to keep them from misusing the truth to damage the President.

As instructed, North replaced the letters "NSC" with "USG" (for U.S. Government) in the chronology. He made some changes of dates, as he was told to do.

McFarlane took North's chronology and made significant revisions. "The most misleading changes to the chronology were made personally by Robert McFarlane," says Judge Silberman.[78]

The false chronology was never used.[79]

Where's the Beef?

You may wonder, if the false chronology was never used, how could North be convicted of aiding and abetting the obstruction of Congress when an obstruction did not take place? That's the beauty of Congress's trap. You do not have to break the law anymore to be a criminal. You can be convicted on a technicality.

Count 6 of the indictment charged that North "unlawfully, willfully and knowingly did *corruptly* influence, obstruct and impede and endeavor to influence, obstruct and impede the *due and proper exercise of the power of inquiry* under which inquiries and investigations were being had by committees of Congress. . . ."[80]

Section 1505 of Congress's law makes it a crime, punishable by a fine or imprisonment, or both, for anyone who "*corruptly*, or by threats of force, or by any threatening letter or communication influences, obstructs, or impedes *or endeavors* to influence, obstruct or impede . . . the *due and proper exercise* of the power of inquiry under which any inquiry or investigation is being had by [Congress]."[81]

All it took was an *uncompleted endeavor* on North's part, even though the chronology was never used. The fact that he followed orders and altered the chronology when it might be used was a crime under federal law. But that is not the whole story.

A "Proper" Exercise of the Power of Inquiry

Under the Founding Fathers' view of separation of powers, the key political question becomes whether Congress was actually involved in a "proper" exercise of their power of inquiry. Under the Framers' view of the Constitution, and as practiced by George Washington who presided over its writing, the President has the right to ask whether or not Congress is inquiring in a "proper" way, namely, in a legally, politically, and ethically fair manner.

If the Executive Branch legitimately and in good faith doubts whether the inquiry is being exercised "properly," and consequently does not fully cooperate, the endeavor to impede cannot be "corrupt" because the President or the executive branch is not acting out of a *bad purpose*.

The Founding Fathers separated the legislative and executive branches specifically for the purpose of causing them to impede each other.[82] They are supposed to impede each other so that one branch does not obtain uncontrolled power.

Neither Congress nor the Courts should assume that the executive branch is "corruptly" endeavoring to impede Congress by the mere fact that it is "endeavoring" to impede Congress. To presume that members of the Executive Branch are criminals for doing what the Constitution equips them to do is ludicrous. To make it illegal for members of the Executive branch to impede Congress in this kind of circumstance violates the separation of powers and unduly enlarges the power of the legislative branch.

The President and the Executive Branch is supposed to be able to check and balance Congress by not responding if, in the President's considered judgment, and not merely as a pretext, *he suspects that the Congress is doing its job improperly or for improper reasons.*[83]

The judge never told the jury to take into consideration North's reasons for questioning whether the inquiry was "proper" or not. The judge never told the jury to consider whether the Executive Branch had valid reasons to question whether the inquiry was politically motivated. North was not allowed to show that, as a member of the President's security staff, he had honorable doubts about the motives of Congress, and that therefore he was *not* acting "corruptly."

Unfortunately, recent Supreme Court cases, particularly within the last thirty years or so, have expanded Congress's power to investigate so broadly that the separation of powers question is no longer considered.[84] The Supreme Court itself has allowed Congress to strip the Executive Branch of this important check and balance.

Thus, when the judge instructed the jury to go for the double whammy on Count 6, he then forbad the jury to consider North's motives, or Congress's. The

District Court's method of determining how to apply Section 1505 embraced the doctrine of parliamentary supremacy. We are back to Star Chamber.

Under judicial rules laid down in federal court cases, Congress can force the executive branch to answer unless the President himself invokes executive privilege. And after Watergate, even invoking privilege is no longer an impenetrable wall. Through numerous cases and judicial rules, the Courts themselves have indicated that they will acquiesce when Congress seizes power by criminalizing policy differences.[85]

The Appeals Court Review

North a Criminal by a Technicality

The Appeals Court seems to have wanted to reverse North's conviction on Count Six but could not because of technicalities. For example, North's attorneys had not expected the trial judge to use Special Verdict forms, therefore they had not taken appropriate steps to the prepare the jury for the aiding and abetting matter. However, case precedents in the D.C. Circuit prohibited the Appeals Court from reversing the convictions despite the fact that these kinds of mistakes had been made.

Second, even though to violate Section 1505 one must have endeavored "corruptly," the Court was prohibited by case precedents from examining North's motives or asking whether he believed he was lawfully authorized.

Factors such as these went straight to the quick of the issue of "corruptly" endeavoring. But technical rules prohibited North from being able to show that his motive was not "corrupt" and therefore that he had not broken the law. It did not matter that he believed that he was following a lawful order in the interests of national security. This is why traps are traps. Once the trap is laid, there is not supposed to be a way out.

The Appeals Court wrestled with the dilemma of having to find North guilty of aiding and abetting "corruption." It opined that

> to assert that <u>all endeavors</u> to influence, obstruct or impede the proceedings of congressional committees are, as a matter of law, corrupt — <u>would undoubtedly criminalize some innocent behavior</u>. . . . [C]ongressional committees are part and parcel of a <u>political branch</u> of government and therefore serve wide-ranging political functions <u>not</u> limited to a search for truth in accordance with formal rules. They may also have a far-flung investigative scope and evoke <u>legitimate political jousting</u> between the executive and legislative branches. No one can seriously question that people constantly attempt, in innumerable ways, to obstruct or impede congressional committees.[86]

The Appeals Court went on to explain that it is <u>not</u> "corrupt" to try to influence, obstruct, or impede Congress. Moreover, to influence, obstruct, or impede Congress is <u>not</u> by definition a "corrupt endeavor." The question was whether North, through his actions, was "endeavoring corruptly."

North's lawyers had understood this to mean that for them to show he was not endeavoring "corruptly," they must prove that he did not have a corrupt motive.[87] The Appeals Court accepted the fact that their evidence showed that he did not have a corrupt motive. The Court ruled, however, that legal precedents and case precedents in the D.C. Circuit made his motives irrelevant. In other words, he could still be found guilty of endeavoring corruptly even if he was not endeavoring corruptly![88]

In the D.C. Circuit, proof of authorization is supposed to be a valid defense. But the case law in the D.C. Circuit on this point is a bit confusing. At the trial, North's lawyers had relied on cases which the Appeals Court later decided it would no longer recognize. By trying to follow the case law of the circuit, and defending North by arguments that were supposed to be valid, North's lawyers failed to make the arguments that they should have because the Appeals Court changed the rules of the game after the game was over. This is a bad way to lose.

Finally, the indictment charged North with "knowingly" violating the law. The trial judge even instructed the jury that he must have "not only acted knowingly, voluntarily, and deliberately, but that he acted with a bad purpose, . . ."[89] To this, North's lawyers demonstrated (to the Appeals Court's satisfaction) that North did not knowingly violate the law.

This should have been enough, right? Wrong. The Appeals Court was obligated to rule, based on their own precedents, that whether he knowingly violated the law was irrelevant. He could be held guilty whether or not he had any knowledge of illegality.[90] Go to jail, Do not pass Go, Do not collect $200.

Judge Silberman's Dissent

Judge Silberman thought that it was simply amazing that the majority refused to reverse North's conviction on Count 6. First, Section 1505 is a "specific intent" criminal law, namely, it requires knowledge of illegality. But the Court ruled that Section 1505 could be violated without knowledge of illegality. Second, North was held guilty of "corruptly endeavoring" even when he was able to show that he was not "corruptly endeavoring."

Third, case law in the circuit had established that if a person was authorized by a superior to do specific deeds, and the employee believed that the superior had the authority to authorize such actions, this could be used to show that the employee was both authorized and lacked a criminal motive or knowledge of illegality.

Since we are dealing here with no ordinary employer, but with the President of the United States, who has the special constitutional authority as well as the duty to resist Congress from time to time, his authorization is on an entirely different level where such criminal laws are concerned than if he were merely the plant foreman down at the brickyard.

Those precedents meant, to Judge Silberman at least, that North should be acquitted if he had been specifically authorized by the President himself to undertake such actions.

North had asked at trial to be allowed to subpoena Reagan, because the President's testimony would show that "as President, he encouraged, approved, authorized, condoned, and at times directed various members of the executive branch to withhold from members of Congress information concerning the sale of arms to Iran as well as information about aid provided to the Contras during the period of the Boland Amendments."[91]

The trial judge refused to subpoena Reagan. North was thus denied the chance to defend himself in a way that should have been permitted under the case law of the D.C. Circuit. His every move was blocked by technicalities.

So on Count 6, where a verdict of not guilty was supposed to end the matter, he was handed the surprise of being convicted of an extra charge of aiding and abetting because the wrong verdict form had been used and because the jury had been given wrong instructions. And the conviction was for *following an order* to help prepare a chronology *that was never used*. (That conviction was vacated on other grounds, however. So justice was finally done, but not the way it could have been.)

NINETEEN

Why the Coup Failed
Congress's Plan Unravels

In the foregoing chapters, I have explained the various parts of the Iran/Contra power grab on the part of Congress, their illegal attainting of Oliver North by means of an *unconstitutional legislative trial*, and their attempt to *set him up* for a criminal conviction in the Courts. The attainting worked; the criminal set up did not. Now that the broad outlines have been painted on the canvass, it is time to fill in a few more of the details.

The Achilles Heel

The entire success of Congress's plan depended on two things. First, they expected the American People and the federal courts to follow the doctrine of Parliamentary supremacy. If the public or the federal courts failed to go along with Congress's view of its unquestioned superiority over the executive branch, the entire attack would fall apart.

Second, they had every reason to believe that the federal courts would allow Congress and the

Independent Counsel to get away with violating the Constitution's Fifth Amendment guarantee of the right not to be a witness against one's self.

The Prosecutor's Case Falls Apart

All went well for the IC at first. Congress had broadcast North's congressional testimony so widely that it was all but impossible for people not to know about it or to come into contact with it. Every grand jury witness was thoroughly immersed in North's testimony. A number of them had been called before Congress to respond specifically to statements that he had made under the so-called grant of immunity.

The grand jury examined not only the truckloads of direct evidence gathered by the IC's investigation, but also heard from witnesses who were intimately familiar with North's testimony. The Grand Jury was never informed about the constitutional issue of separation of powers. They were simply commanded to follow the IC's view of criminal law, one that was skewed, perverse, and unconstitutional. The indictments were a cinch. Walsh got them easily.

But then the problems began. The indictment against McFarlane, and the 23 Count indictment against Poindexter, North, Secord and Hakim rested on a criminal conspiracy theory which was itself premised on the notion of parliamentary supremacy.

This posed a serious problem for Walsh. To obtain the indictments, Walsh had convinced the Grand Jury that North and friends had *criminally conspired* to violate the Arms Export Control Act, the Boland Amendments and two executive orders which had been issued by President Reagan.[92] But Walsh knew that these allegations would not hold up in court.

First, the missiles belonged to Israel, were shipped from Israel, had Israeli markings on them, and did not violate the Arms Export Control Act at all.

Second, North and friends had not factually violated the Boland Amendments and could prove it. They had not used U.S. Treasury appropriations. Third, the Boland Amendments were probably unconstitutional as an intrusion into the power of the presidency, and therefore violating them would be inconsequential.

Fourth, even if they had violated the Boland Amendments, they could show that it was ***within the President's constitutional authority*** to circumvent the amendments on other constitutional grounds. If Walsh brought this charge into court, the case would probably be thrown out on the first day. He had no Boland Amendment case! He did not dare charge them with violating the Boland Amendment, because he was certain to lose on that point.

Similarly, he had learned that North and Poindexter were following orders both on the Iran initiative and in their support of the Contras. Walsh could not win on the criminal conspiracy charge that they violated the President's orders because they were able to show for both of the larger operations that they were following the President's orders.

Walsh realized that the main support pillars for his entire criminal conspiracy case had collapsed as if tumbled to pieces by Samson. So he dropped the first four counts of the indictment.[93] He never charged

North with violating the Arms Export Control Act or any other laws regarding the shipments to Iran. And, he never charged North with violating the Boland Amendments.

Instead he charged North with the "crime" of not telling Congress what he was doing with respect to the Iran or the Nicaraguan initiatives, and of illegally and intentionally deceiving Congress on both.[94] But the entire foundation for his ingenious story of the purported "criminal Enterprise" evaporated right out from under him. There was no conspiracy.

The Box Canyon Strategy

The Boland Amendments were only the bait anyway, remember? They were the "game scent" used by Congress *to lure the President and his men into the contempt of Congress and the impeding Congress trap*. It did not matter that a separation of powers argument might defeat the Boland Amendments. In the court system there is no separation of powers argument that will defeat a charge of obstructing Congress or of lying to Congress.[95]

Congress had the Executive Branch trapped in the proverbial box canyon. The President had a duty to help the Contras. The Congress forbad him to help the Contras. The President began helping Contras anyway (which was legal). Then the Congress demanded that the President and his men tell Congress what they were doing.

If the President told Congress what he was doing, they could exercise their vast lawmaking power, investigatory power, and regulatory control over the various branches of government to stop him. *The American people would not realize that by doing so, Congress would be usurping the President's foreign affairs power.*

If Reagan invoked executive privilege to keep from answering, or if he ordered North not to answer, Congress would cry "coverup." The Watergate Pox would strike and Reagan would be finished as President.

And if his men said nothing, or said the wrong thing, Congress's law about full disclosure would immediately come into play. Once Congress demanded an answer from them, even silence or foot dragging on their part would be a crime under modern law.

This situation exists because the Supreme Court and the various federal courts have embraced the fallacy of parliamentary supremacy in this area of the criminal law dealing with congressional investigations. For over thirty years, the federal courts have ruled that anyone who fails under oath to answer a question fully and completely when asked by Congress is *strictly liable for being found a criminal regardless of his intent or motive*. The rule also applies to the executive branch, despite the doctrine of separation of powers.

It does not matter that North had a constitutional right, as a member of the President's staff, not to answer or to give an evasive or even misleading answer in this kind of situation. The federal courts no longer recognize that right. After Congress placed this "Star Chamber" inquisition law on the books the federal courts have upheld it vigorously. Congress knew this, and so did Walsh. Walsh had North cornered.

The Perjury Trap

McFarlane, North, and Poindexter were in a no win situation. They were not permitted to keep silent when placed under oath by Congress. But to tell the Congress the truth would cost innocent people their lives. To tell Congress the truth would be to forfeit another chunk of the President's constitutional powers to the Congress as well.

But to be evasive under oath, when Congress had the uncontested power to subpoena their records, would make them fall into the perjury trap. Any man who talks long enough will eventually correct himself or even contradict himself. But it is perjury to contradict yourself, even innocently, when under oath.[96]

Moreover, it is only a slight elaboration to note, somewhat humorously, that three eyewitnesses to the same car wreck will have four different versions of what happened. Consequently, Congress's grant of immunity was no real protection for North (which Congress knew all along).

He could still be found guilty of perjury if someone else testified differently under oath than he did, and if the Court believed the other person's recollection rather than North's. The ability to make someone a perjurer is extremely easy. The perjury trap is one of Congress's and prosecutors' favorite bludgeons for clubbing people into submission.

It certainly worked on McFarlane. He testified against North at trial pursuant to a plea agreement with the prosecutor's office.

The Good Fight

North courageously argued to the court the constitutional grounds for the President's control of foreign policy, knowing that they would be rejected. They were. The trial judge agreed with Walsh that foreign policy is set by Congress.

In ruling on North's motions to dismiss, Judge Gesell said "The gist of North's motions to dismiss reveals a skewed attitude toward our form of constitutional government. . . . There is nothing in the Constitution, federal statutes or applicable decisions which warrants this cynical approach. This Court must reject it totally."[97]

The good judge issued scathing blasts against North's challenges to the lynching that was taking place. As the judge's preliminary rulings indicate, Congress and the Prosecutor were right to be confident that the case law was squarely against North on almost every alleged point.

The judge even announced North's guilt before there was a trial. He had prejudged North. In denying North's motion to dismiss Counts 5, 6, and 7, Judge Gesell said that North had "affirmatively deceived Congress, . . . He cannot claim any sort of privilege for this. . . . Such a disdainful view of our democratic form of government has no constitutional substance."[98]

North's separation of powers arguments fell on deaf ears as well. When he tried to persuade the judge that the Executive Branch should have an equal role with Congress in establishing the policies affecting the Executive Branch, *the judge opted for the parliamentary supremacy approach*, saying: "Whatever the practice, Congress has not accepted North's policy contentions, and Congress has set the standard."[99]

What the Heck is CIPA?

The backyard barbecuing of Colonel North was right on schedule. Everything was working out just as Congress had planned . . . until the judge started dealing with the classified documents.

Another part of the trap laid by Congress was the Classified Information Procedures Act. The CIPA law requires a defendant to tell the prosecutor which classified documents he intends to use in his own defense and requires him to tell the prosecutor the reasons for which he will use the documents!

This means, of course, that for the defendant like Oliver North, whose entire case rests upon information in top secret documents, to comply with CIPA he has to reveal his entire case to the very person whose job it is to put him behind bars! The Independent Counsel had been unfair to North every step of the way. Now the law required North to rely on the good faith of the prosecutor for a fair trial. Fat chance.

CIPA also provides, that if the government does not want the actual document to be used, it can offer the court a summary of the document, called a "redaction," to be used instead. Government employees with security clearances sit as a redaction committee to decide what classified information will be allowed and what will not be allowed. If the Court authorizes certain documents to be used in evidence, the Prosecutor has the right under CIPA to demand that summaries be used instead.

North had no control over whether the summaries were accurate or not.[100] Many of the documents he requested were not made available to him. Instead, he was offered "redactions," and was required to agree with the government's summary of what was in those classified documents. Does that sound fair to you?

The outcome of the trial turned on the contents of thousands of classified documents. Neither the judge nor the prosecutor knew the secret codes, keywords, or interpretations for many of those documents. They needed North to tell them what the documents were and what they meant!

On June 22, 1988, Judge Gesell ordered North to disclose by July 11 which classified documents and information he intended to use in his own defense. Since it takes more than a few weeks to go through 900,000 documents to find the ones you're looking for (they were no longer in proper order after being shipped across town), North asked for an extension. He was granted until August 1, 1988 to make the disclosure.

North filed his disclosure on August 1. Judge Gesell was furious that North had not laid out the particulars for his use of certain information. He rejected North's disclosure as wholly insufficient and ordered him to make another disclosure by November 14, 1988.

North made the disclosure on time, but still did not give away the substance of his case to the prosecutor, contrary to what both the judge and the prosecutor expected. *North knew he was getting shafted.*

As a punishment for North's "deliberate disregard of the Court's Order," Judge Gesell gave North until January 3, 1989 to select only 300 classified documents to be used in his defense. Under the order, North would explain to Judge Gesell in private, with the prosecutor absent, his reasons for using the documents. He would also file an outline or "narrative summary" with the judge, explaining the details to the judge but not to the prosecutor.

On December 19, 1988, North filed a 162 page narrative summary of his case privately before the judge. It explained in detail how North intended to use the classified information for his defense. The prosecutor ***was not present*** to hear North's defense strategy. Four days later, Judge Gesell ordered North to give the summary to the prosecutor. Sounds really fair doesn't it?

North asked the judge to cause the prosecutor to make available the evidence he intended to use to rebut North's information. The CIPA law required this disclosure to be made to North. But the judge refused to require it, and the prosecutor never handed over to North the information he was supposed to give.[101] So much for an impartial judge and due process!

As Judge Silberman pointed out, "North was required to disclose an enormous portion of his case, under a regime where he got nothing in return."[102] The Supreme Court, in the Wardius case, had said that in trials involving CIPA, the defendant cannot be forced to disclose elements of his case unless he receives from the prosecutor the evidence to be used to refute the disclosed elements.[103] Too bad. North was ***supposed*** to lose. That is the whole point. The fix was in from the beginning.

That Dang Jury

Despite this monumental judicial error of constitutional proportions, which was *not* reversed on Appeal, North still prevailed before the jury on almost every Count. Although the Prosecutor tried to stack the deck against North with the CIPA law, and even though North was unfairly *forced to reveal his defense strategy*, the classified information supported what North had been saying all along.

The judge had forced North to give leads and strategy ideas to the prosecutor. The government had withheld key information for which North had asked, or only gave him inadequate summaries of certain key documents which were crucial to his defense. The Prosecutor had manipulated the grand jury and the district court trial. Despite all this, North prevailed on most of the counts, a compellingly impressive victory.

Remember, he was never charged with violating the Boland Amendments. He was never charged with violating any law regarding arms shipments to Iran. And he, personally, was never charged with lying to Congress! Get the picture?

He was accused of making false statements in letters that Robert McFarlane had instructed him to write. The jury acquitted him on every Count of making false statements![104] The jury was forced, *by technicalities* and mistakes made by the trial judge to convict him of destroying documents. The jury by technicalities and mistakes made by the trial judge found him guilty of aiding and abetting the obstruction of Congress. His sole crime in the end was in receiving a security fence that cost more than $100.

Because of all the mistaken and inflammatory reporting by the media and misleading political rhetoric from politicians, many people believe that Colonel North was convicted of lying to Congress about his support for the Contras. Wrong!

The aiding and abetting conviction, which was later overturned, dealt with the Israeli missile shipment in November 1985! North was never convicted of lying to Congress about his activities in support of the Contras. In fact, he was never convicted of lying to Congress period!

When all is said and done, Iran/Contra boils down to a $100 million dollar effort on the part of Congress and the Special Prosecutor to bring down the Reagan presidency and then the Bush presidency because Oliver North received a security fence. That's sad.

McFarlane, North's boss and advisor to the President, was the one charged with lying to Congress. After McFarlane had pled guilty (when he should not have) he wrote a letter to the sentencing judge to tell him: "The fact that I acted under the guidance and emphatic instructions of the President is, I recognize, irrelevant." But as Richmond attorney Joseph Blackburn, who read all 1,000 pages of McFarlane's trial testimony, pointed out, "Since when is acting under the guidance and emphatic instructions of the President of the United States irrelevant?"[105]

TWENTY

The Wheels of Justice

The Appeals Court Calls a Halt

It's time to put to rest, once and for all, the prevailing myths about the Appeals Court's reasons for overturning the guilty verdicts. The enemies and detractors of Oliver North continue to insist that the Appeals Court "let him off on a technicality."

The truth is that the Appeals Court called a halt to an unconstitutional charade whereby Oliver North was given the *semblance* of a judicial trial, but only as a *subterfuge*. The process had been rigged from the start by Congress and the Independent Counsel to achieve a *predetermined outcome*. If the American people see this as merely a technicality, heaven help us.

I have already shown that, despite the extraordinary efforts of the prosecutor to the contrary, the jury found North "Not Guilty" on every count of false statements to Congress, "Not Guilty" on every Count of obstructing Congress, and "Not Guilty" of obstructing a presidential investigation.

It found him guilty of destroying documents. But this verdict was reversed because the judge gave the jury the wrong instructions, requiring a guilty verdict when no law was broken.

The jury found North guilty of receiving a security fence, which was a stupid and cynical reason to have a trial in the first place. (As Judge Silberman noted, the fence was not a payoff for political favors.) And, finally, the jury found him guilty of aiding and abetting the obstruction of Congress for redrafting a chronology of events in the shipment of missiles to Iran, even though the chronology was never used.

The Real Conspiracy

Bait and Switch

The decision to reverse the conviction on Count 9 and to send the three verdicts back to trial was the Appeals Court's way of telling Congress and the Independent Counsel that enough is enough. The real conspiracy had been on the part of those who were trashing the Constitution to destroy North and to pick off Reagan's associates one at a time.

Congress had the perfect plan for "getting around" the Constitution. It was the old "bait and switch" tactic. It would pretend to protect North's Fifth Amendment right not to testify against himself by "granting him immunity." This supposedly would stop the prosecutor from using North's testimony as evidence either in the grand jury or later in the hoped for criminal trial.

But by holding widely televised public hearings Congress could insure that members of the grand jury, members of the trial jury, prosecuting attorneys, and witnesses would be exposed to his testimony.

By blanketing the country with North's "protected testimony," Congress hoped to influence the grand jury so that it would surely hand down an indictment. Because North's testimony would be everywhere – Washington would be soaked in it – the prosecutors would surely know how to frame their arguments, know which witnesses to interrogate, and which legal strategies to follow.

In this devious way, North's testimony would definitely get before the grand jury and before the trial jury without being presented to them directly by North himself or by the Special Counsel. It was the perfect trap.

Walsh had 68 lawyers and hundreds of investigators working for him over the course of the investigation. He also had 112 paralegals, secretaries, technicians, and other staff working for him. They would have to live on Mars not to come into repeated contact with North's testimony or those who were soaked in North's testimony.

This contact would assist the lawyers in focusing the investigation, deciding whether to initiate prosecutions, whether to accept or refuse plea bargains, how to interpret evidence, how to plan cross-examinations, and in general how to plan trial strategy.[106]

By making North's testimony "ubiquitous," everywhere and ever present, Congress would give the prosecutors a knowledge of the immunized testimony which might help them interpret evidence previously unintelligible to them, and expose as significant facts once thought irrelevant, or vice versa. Exposure to the testimony might indicate to the prosecutors which witnesses to call, and in what order. And the compelled testimony might be helpful to them in developing their opening or closing arguments.[107]

Congress's plan was to manipulate the system in such a way that the prosecutor would be able to use North's immunized testimony without appearing to be using the testimony. The Prosecutor's plan was to make full use of the opportunity.

Since the trial judge had prejudged North as a criminal, and was sympathetic to Walsh (himself a judge and part of the fraternity), he was "similarly untroubled by allegations of prosecutorial exposure to the immunized testimony through a grand juror or a witness."[108]

Congress's immunity trap left North totally dependent on the good faith of the prosecutors for the preservation of his constitutional rights. The Appeals Court could not stomach what it saw. It called a halt.

It's Not Over Till It's Over

More importantly, the Appeals Court did "let him off." The Special Prosecutor had another shot. The Appeals Court simply sent the three counts back to the trial judge so that fair processes would be followed before any guilty verdict could be handed down. That is hardly letting somebody off on a technicality.

The Appeals Court strongly believed that North's Fifth Amendment Rights had been violated, both at the grand jury and before the trial jury. It ordered further proceedings, for the sake of fairness, to make sure that the Fifth Amendment was not violated any further.

Chief Judge Patricia Wald (Sister Parliamentary Supremacy herself), believed that North was guilty and was confident that he had received a fair trial (because his "crimes" "had far flung implications for national policy."[109])

Judge Wald dissented from the majority's opinion. It had been her job to monitor the grand jury proceedings to make sure that they were 'fair.' She argued that there was plenty of evidence to convict North despite his immunized testimony. She could not figure what the big fuss was all about.

She talked about the two volumes of "leads." These were detailed interviews of more than eighty major players in Iran/Contra conducted by the FBI in late 1986 and early 1987 before Colonel North had been granted immunity.

She explained that "[e]ven more extensive evidence, compiled by the IC before North's immunized testimony, was 'separated and sealed to ensure a full record of [the IC's] independent development of facts and witnesses should that be necessary in more detail at a further post-trial *Kastigar* hearing.'"[110] Supposedly, "the great bulk of the evidence was clearly known to Independent Counsel before any defendant received use immunity."[111]

She insisted that "nearly all of the grand jury witnesses testifying with regard to Counts 6, 9, and 10 appeared before North presented his immunized testimony to Congress."[112] She accepted the Independent Counsel's assertion that "the testimony relevant to Counts 6, 9, and 10 was presented before North's immunized testimony."[113]

If she was right, then what was the problem? Why did the Independent Counsel, who had no qualms about spending millions of dollars, not wish to go back to the trial Court for further proceedings? If the IC and the trial judge had all the evidence they needed, why not continue? The answer is simple. Walsh knew that he could not win on the guilty verdicts if a fair process was used.

Instead, after the Appeals Court delivered its 62 page opinion, Walsh asked for a rehearing. The Appeals Court issued a second opinion, rebuking Walsh, and explaining more pointedly the reasons for overturning the guilty verdicts.

> When all is said and done, the district judge denied the defendant a hearing to which the Constitution entitled him. The Chief Judge's new formulation of constitutional law does appear to justify that denial, but we think it does so only by subordinating the defendant's constitutional rights to various other interests.[114]

Walsh reluctantly returned to the trial court. But it was no use, so he decided to quit while he was ahead. On September 16, 1991, Walsh asked Judge Gesell to enter an order dismissing all charges against North. For Walsh it was time to cut his losses and move on. Walsh himself dropped the charges. North was not let off on a technicality by the courts.

TWENTY-ONE

Abolishing Star Chamber

Congress's September Surprise

Congress never expected the Appeals Court to rain on their parade. Congress had granted North immunity insincerely believing that the Courts would turn a blind eye to Congress's disregard for the Fifth Amendment and the Prosecutor's use of compelled testimony. Up until now, the federal courts had not applied a rigorous standard.

But the Appeals Court was flabbergasted. What had happened with North, from the televised hearings, through the grand jury, to the trial was in the Court's words an "unprecedented aberration."[115] The Appeals Court realized that the old abuses of Star Chamber had been revived. The attack against North was precisely the same kind of *medieval* chicanery that had given rise to the Fifth Amendment in the first place. Here is where the line had to be drawn.

The Fifth Amendment

The Constitution guarantees that "No person . . . shall be compelled in any criminal case to be a witness against himself. . . ." Over 100 years ago the Supreme Court had explained this to mean:

> And any compulsory discovery by extorting the party's oath, or compelling the production of his private books and papers, to convict him of crime, or to forfeit his property, is contrary to the principles of free government. It is abhorrent to the instincts of an Englishman; it is abhorrent to the instincts of an American. It may suit the purposes of despotic power; but it cannot abide the pure atmosphere of political liberty and personal freedom.[116]

The Appeals Court took seriously the violation of the Fifth Amendment, saying: "Such compulsion is an ageless badge of tyranny, one that framers and ratifiers of the Constitution were determined to avoid."[117]

Congress got around this restriction by enacting what is known as the Federal Use Immunity Statute.[118] Now, by granting "immunity" from the use of one's testimony, Congress can order a witness to testify rather than keep silent, and consequently make him look like a criminal when he is not.

Congress beats the answers out of it victims, not with hot lights and rubber hoses, but with hot lights and rubber-shielded video cables. It torments its enemies by sentencing them to slow death by media feeding frenzy. Congress dooms whom it despises to a modern analogy of medieval water torture, where one is deprived of sanity and security by the incessant drip, drip, drip of scandal, rumor, suspicion and innuendo. Congress does not break its victims on the wheel. Rather it breaks them *on the satellite dish of the sky-cam truck*.

The Use Immunity Statute was challenged before the United States Supreme Court. The Court, in the *Kastigar* case, said that the statute was constitutional as long as the compelled testimony could not be used in any way that violated the Fifth Amendment.[119]

The Problem With "Use" Immunity

From Watergate to "Kastigate"

Here is the problem with the "Use" Immunity Statute. It treats the issue of compelled testimony as if the Bill of Attainder Clause is not in the Constitution. This is precisely why in 1987 Congress thought it could get around the Constitution and attaint Oliver North.

The Fifth Amendment promises only that a man will not be forced to testify against himself in a *criminal* trial. But the Fifth Amendment does not exist in isolation. It has as its companion the Bill of Attainder clause that protects one from testifying against himself before Congress so that the legislature cannot destroy his *reputation* in the community.[120]

In the situation where Congress forces a person to testify publicly in answer to criminal accusations, without the Bill of Attainder clause the protection provided by the Fifth Amendment is incomplete. That is why the framers put them both in one Constitution. They complement each other. But we have forgotten.

Congress wanted to compel North to testify in order to make him look like a criminal and consequently be ruined in eyes of the community *regardless* of what happened in court. That strategy by Congress was unconstitutional as a bill of attainder.

As the Supreme Court said in the Apfelbaum case, the Fifth Amendment privilege against self-incrimination "does not extend to consequences of a *noncriminal* nature, such as threats of liability in civil suits, disgrace in the community, or loss of employment."[121]

Which is precisely the point. The Fifth Amendment, standing alone, offered no protection to North or to anyone else for that matter who was compelled to testify before the unconstitutional legislative inquisition in the summer of 1987. Compelling North to testify before Congress violated the bill of attainder clause more than the Fifth Amendment. As the Appeals Court pointed out:

> North does not contend that the government violated his Fifth Amendment right because he received bad press as a result of his immunized testimony, or that he has been unable to find employment. Rather, he protests that the government used his immunized testimony to secure his indictment and subsequent conviction as a federal felon.[122]

If a man can be forced to testify in answer to criminal accusations at a legislative hearing, he can be attainted in the community even if he is not convicted as a criminal in the courts. This was Congress's *punitive strategy* against Oliver North all along. And it worked only too well.

The Double-Dip

Congress thought it could get North both ways. It could "double-dip" him, both with a ruined reputation, and also with a criminal conviction. Congress believed it could achieve this result because America had forgotten the bill of attainder clause, and the lower federal courts had gutted the supposed protections of the "Use" Immunity Statute.

The lower courts had made exceptions to both the Fourth and Fifth Amendments "for the proposition that recollection may be refreshed with inadmissible evidence even when the government violated the Fourth and Fifth Amendments to obtain the evidence."[123]

These case opinions gave Walsh the carte blanche permission to violate the Constitution at will and with impunity in order to "get" Oliver North, Ronald Reagan, and anyone else involved with the Iran initiative and the Nicaraguan initiative.

So even though the Supreme Court had ruled that the coerced testimony could not be used, the lower courts had found a way to use it! *This was as if someone had taken a black magic marker and crossed the Fifth Amendment right out of the Constitution*. It also meant that the Use Immunity Statute as interpreted by the lower courts was itself a violation of Article 1, Section 9, Clause 3 of the Constitution.

Congress fully expected North's testimony to reach both the grand jury and the trial jury. Congress also fully expected not to be stopped by the federal courts from doing so. When the Appeals Court handed down a decision to the contrary, it came as an immense surprise.

The Washington Post reported on September 17, 1991, that when Congress was told about the Appeals Court's opinion and Walsh's decision to dismiss all charges against Oliver North, "House leaders defended [their immunity grant decision] saying they could not have foreseen the subsequent change in legal standards governing tainted testimony."[124] See what I mean?

Torquemada's Inquisition

Walsh had made full use of the courts' gutting of the Fifth Amendment. During the grand jury phase, Walsh systematically excluded from the grand jury any evidence that would exculpate Oliver North. Walsh did whatever it took to obtain those indictments.

He gave the grand jury erroneous legal instructions and misleading interpretations of the Constitution. He hammered home the fallacy of parliamentary supremacy. And, among other violations, he allowed unauthorized persons to be present in violation of the federal rules of procedure. But, despite North's protests, the trial judge refused to quash the indictment because Chief Judge Patricia Wald had monitored all the proceedings. How touching.

But the Appeals Court would have none of it. They were not about to sanction this modern corollary to Star Chamber.

> Yet the very purpose of the Fifth Amendment under these circumstances is to prevent the prosecutor from transmogrifying into the inquisitor, complete with that officer's most pernicious tool – the power of the state to force a person to incriminate himself. As between the clear constitutional command and the convenience of the government, our duty is to enforce the former and discount the latter.[125]

The problem with Inquisitors is that they can "create" criminals because they control a process that is fixed from the beginning. "Heads I win, tails you lose." It was not that North was made a criminal because he had confessed to crimes or that his answers incriminated him. The problem was that the process was rigged to make his deeds appear to be crimes whether they were or not!

Had North been found guilty by a jury after due process of law and without ever having been attainted by the Congress of the United States, I would not have written this book. He should have been investigated, tried by a jury of his peers, and convicted according to law. As it was, he came close to being completely exonerated despite the incredibly unjust process that was used against him – despite the fact that the deck had been stacked by Congress itself at the cost of millions of dollars. In my humble opinion, had justice been done according to law, the IC *would never have obtained an indictment in the first place*.

And again, that is precisely the point. Congress knew that unless a phony, unconstitutional, unjust procedure was followed, there never would have been an indictment on which North could be convicted anyway. He would never, never, never have been judged a felon, period. They had to *rig the system* to reach their unconstitutional goal.

This Was a "Political" Trial

No Judicial Due Process of Law

The key question in the eyes of the Appeals Court was "whether the prosecution's case made *use* of North's compelled testimony" because "we do not countenance political trials in this country, . . ."[126] The Appeals Court was disgusted by the Prosecutor's use before the grand jury and at trial of North's compelled testimony – with the trial judge's permission – because "[P]resenting the testimony of grand jury or trial witnesses that has been derived from or influenced by the immunized testimony . . . [is] forbidden" by the Fifth Amendment.[127]

Before the grand jury and at the trial, "witnesses had their memories refreshed with the immunized testimony by 'hearing the testimony, reading about it, being questioned about aspects of it before the Select Committees and, to some extent by exposure to it in the course of responding to inquiries with their respective agencies.'"[128]

The IC, the trial judge, and Chief Judge Patricia Wald insisted that this "use" was not "use." But the Appeals Court majority answered.

> In our view, the use of immunized testimony by witnesses to refresh their memories, or otherwise

> to focus their thoughts, organize their testimony, or alter their prior or contemporaneous statements, constitutes . . . use. This observation also applies to witnesses who studied, reviewed, or were exposed to the immunized testimony in order to prepare themselves or others as witnesses. . . . When the government puts on witnesses who refresh, supplement, or modify that evidence with compelled testimony, the government uses that testimony to indict and convict. The fact that the government violates the Fifth Amendment in a circuitous or haphazard fashion is cold comfort to the citizen who has been forced to incriminate himself by threat of imprisonment for contempt.[129]

Witnesses had studied North's testimony in order to be ready to testify. Some were for him, some were not. But with the guillotine blade of criminal convictions hoisted precariously over everyone's neck, the incentive was strong for witnesses to study North's testimony so that they could give answers which would make him the scapegoat and absolve themselves. That is why due process of law was entirely lacking in these proceedings. Self-interest would to some degree influence every witness to try to make North a criminal in order to save themselves.

Applying the Brakes

To Congress, the Trial Court, and the IC

By overturning the verdicts and sending the case

back to the lower court for further hearings, the Appeals Court was trying to do a repair job on the Fifth Amendment without having to rule that the Immunized Testimony law was unconstitutional. Along the way the Court gave some clear rebukes to Congress, the trial judge, and the Independent Counsel . . . in judicial language, of course, but rebukes nonetheless. First it laid out the nature of the problem, and why the Fifth Amendment had been violated:

> A central problem in this case is that many grand jury and trial witnesses were thoroughly soaked in North's immunized testimony, but no effort was made to determine what effect, if any, this extensive exposure had on their testimony. Papers filed under seal indicate that officials and attorneys from the Department of Justice, the Central Intelligence Agency, the White House, and the Department of State gathered, studied, and summarized North's immunized testimony in order to prepare themselves or their superiors and colleagues for their testimony before the investigating committees and the grand jury.[130]
>
> The testimony of Robert C. McFarlane, the National Security Advisor to President Reagan, is especially troubling and is indeed emblematic of both the weakness of the IC's position and the necessity of further *Kastigar* inquiry. Although McFarlane completed his grand jury testimony *before* North gave his immunized

> testimony, McFarlane was a key government witness at trial. He testified before the investigating committees prior to North's immunized testimony, but then *specifically requested and was granted a second appearance* after North testified in order to respond to North's testimony. . . . In his second appearance on Capitol Hill, McFarlane revised his earlier testimony in light of North's testimony at certain points. . . . He also apparently managed to recall items that he had not remembered in his prior testimony.[131]

Rebuke to Walsh

The Appeals Court realized that Walsh had violated the Constitution. But judicial etiquette required the Court to send the case back for another hearing on that point, rather than finding as a matter of law that the violation took place. The message to Walsh was unambiguous, however. He had led a wild stampede, hooves a flying, trampling the Constitution into the dust on his way to gore Oliver North.

The inference was unmistakable: "When the government [i.e., Walsh] puts on witnesses who . . . modify that evidence with compelled testimony, the government [i.e., Walsh] violates the Fifth Amendment. . . ."[132]

Just as Congress had rejected all of Oliver North's pleas not to be subjected to a mock political trial, the district judge had rejected all of North's requests to honor the Fifth Amendment. Consequently Walsh proceeded merrily on his way to North's conviction.

The Appeals Court, however, reminded Walsh that "[w]here immunized testimony is used before a grand jury" the prosecutor himself is the wrongdoer. "[T]he prohibited act is simultaneous and coterminous with the presentation; indeed they are one and the same."[133] "[T]he wrong use of [the immunized testimony] goes to the quick of the indictment."[134]

The Appeals Court warned that it had the power to "look behind and dismiss an indictment where there is a strong likelihood that the grand jury process itself violated the witness's fifth amendment privilege."[135]

Rebuke to the Trial Judge

The Appeals Court was *especially critical* of the conduct of the trial judge: "[The] District Court . . . made no determination of the extent to which the substantive content of the witnesses' testimony may have been shaped, altered, or affected by the immunized testimony."[136] And, he was "similarly untroubled by allegations of prosecutorial exposure to the immunized testimony through a grand juror or a witness."[137]

Because the trial judge shared Congress's view of Parliamentary supremacy, and he shared the view of both Congress and Walsh that North's testimony could be used, he did not rely on any of the "canned" testimony which was gathered prior to North's appearance before Congress.

The Appeals Court was appalled that the materials which had been gathered before North testified played no part in the District Court's review. The materials had been filed with the District Court and were then transferred back to the Independent Counsel to preserve them.

Only *after* the convictions did North have access to any of the grand jury testimony, and then only so much of it that related to the three counts on which he was convicted.[138] It was fair alright, just like Star Chamber was fair.

The Appeals Court reviewed in detail the practical reasons and principles why it was wrong for a court to use such testimony, and then said "These observations have indeed proven prescient, and we commend them to the District Court on remand."[139] That is a polite, judicial way of saying, 'do it right next time, or else.'

Rebuke to Congress

In judicial language, the Court lectured Congress not to use this tactic again. Congress must not think that granting immunity, and then overcoming that grant with a barrage of public exposure, will work any more before the D.C. Circuit.[140]

Summary of North I

Congress, the trial judge, and the Independent Counsel all believed that it was alright to employ an indirect, scattergun-blast method to use Oliver North's testimony against him, when the pretended promise had been that it would not be. By placing North in the immunity trap in the summer of 1987, Congress rigged the system to guarantee that he would go to jail for contempt if he did not testify, and that he would go to jail as a convicted felon if he did testify. And most Americans never knew that this little game was being played. Congress thinks we are so dumb. And we were.

The Appeals Court said loud and clear, it will not tolerate the profaning of the Fifth Amendment: "[T]he use of immunized testimony — before the grand jury or at trial — to augment or refresh recollection is an evidentiary use and must be dealt with as such."[141] No longer will courts and prosecutors in D.C. be allowed to use immunized testimony on the technicality that they claim not to be using it.

The danger to an accused defendant like Oliver North "is a real one in a case such as this where the immunized testimony is so broadly disseminated that interested parties study it and even casual observers have some notion of its content."[142]

The Federal Court system is set up to allow a lower judge to save face when he is wrong. So even though the Appeals Court strongly believed that the government had violated North's fundamental, enumerated constitutional right not to incriminate himself, they sent the case back to the trial judge to fix the problem by giving North a "fair" chance rather than allowing him to be convicted with soviet-styled justice where you are guilty-as-charged, because-I-say-so, case closed.[143]

The "District Court did not even claim to examine the grand jury transcripts for the presence of immunized testimony in the *substance* of the witnesses' testimony."[144] The District Court's summary conclusion that North's testimony was not unconstitutionally used before the grand jury was a "legally erroneous finding concerning grand jury testimony, an approach that is flawed for the reasons noted above."[145]

The Appeals Court hammered the point home by saying that when a prosecutor uses immunized testimony before a grand jury, "the grand jury process itself is violated and corrupted, and the indictment becomes indistinguishable from the constitutional and statutory transgression [by the prosecutor]."[146]

When this happens, the prosecutors and the judges are the ones who are violating the law, and not just any law. They are violating the Constitution itself. The Appeals Court sarcastically remarked that "This distinction eludes the I[ndependent] C[ounsel] and the District Court; . . ."[147]

Because North's testimony had been widely disseminated this threatened to make "the grand jury no longer a grand jury" according to the Appeals Court. It could have caused the dismissal of the indictment out of hand. The Appeals Court decided not to take so severe a route, but allowed the lower court to save face by holding further hearings. As it turned out, those hearings were never completed.

North II

Walsh was not content to follow the Appeals Court's order to go back for further proceedings in the trial court. Instead, he challenged the Appeals Court to change its decision. The Appeals Court was not amused. Their "second opinion" which was handed down three months later was even more blunt.

Walsh tried to convince the Court that it had misread the law about the Fifth Amendment. He wanted the Court to change its mind and to allow the immunized testimony to be used. To which the Court retorted:

> The IC thus continues to miss the fundamental distinction between the presentation to the grand jury of evidence that has previously been unconstitutionally obtained and that of constitutionally-obtained evidence whose exposure to the grand jury amounts to a constitutional violation in and of itself.[148]

Walsh still refused to get the picture that he was the one breaking the law. Walsh was arrogantly and highhandedly violating the Constitution itself in his jaundiced attempt to punish Oliver North for being a threat to democracy for accepting a security fence.

The Court took pains to explain that it violates the Constitution to use testimony that *per se* was excluded by law from being presented to the grand jury. This was no technicality. North was simply treated unfairly and unconstitutionally. The Court concluded by saying: "When all is said and done, the district judge [and the Independent Counsel] denied the defendant a hearing to which the Constitution entitled him."[149]

The critics of Oliver North would have us believe that this is only a technicality. They would have us believe that the Constitution – for which North fought and bled, for which he repeatedly faced death and danger, and faced even the threat of terrorist assassination – protects everyone in America except Oliver North.

TWENTY-TWO

Prosecutorial Misconduct

A Catalog of Excesses and Abuses

The Ethics in Government Act of 1982 was the tool whereby Congress and the Independent Counsel attainted Oliver North and many others in clear defiance of the Constitution of the United States.

The Independent Counsel law itself violates the Bill of Attainder clause of the Constitution by giving the government the power to publish criminal accusations and conclusions of guilt regardless of whether those conclusions were tried in a court of law, or whether they were disproved in a court of law.

Section 595 of the "law to get Reagan" reads:

> (a)(1) independent counsel appointed under this chapter may make public from time to time, and shall send to Congress statements or reports on the activities of such independent counsel. These statements and reports shall contain such information as such independent counsel deems appropriate.

> (b)(3) The division of the court may release to the Congress, the public, or to any appropriate person, such portions of a report made under this subsection as the division deems appropriate.

Before Walsh filed his report with the U.S. Court of Appeals, he had previously made four public reports. At the request of the Society of Professional Journalists, the Court ordered the Final Report to be made public according to Congress's law.

Through this circuitous process, Congress's Bill of Attainder was finally and fully published. The Court did, however, permit those affected to file rebuttals which were published in Volume 3 of the Report.

Those rebuttals, summarized below, catalog a long train of abuses and usurpations committed on the part of the Independent Counsel's office, to harass the enemies of the dominant political party of Congress, and to eat out their substance, and to subject them to a jurisdiction that is foreign to the form of government guaranteed by the Constitution of the United States. This chapter provides the summary of those alleged abuses to a candid world.

Response of Elliot Abrams

- The report selectively uses facts to support the IC's own actions rather than presenting a full and accurate picture. The IC omits quotes from documents and testimony that disprove the IC's accusations of Abrams's criminal activity.[150]

- The report is filled with assertions of facts that are baseless or are at best highly debatable.[151]

- The IC moved against Elliot Abrams only because Walsh had lost his case against Oliver North, and appeared almost certainly to lose the conviction of Poindexter. Abrams had no financial resources. He was an easy target and was coerced into pleading guilty to a plea-bargained misdemeanor which he did not commit, to avoid being set up for a felony conviction which he had no means to resist.

Ambassador Richard Armitage

- "I protest the action of the Independent Counsel in characterizing me as guilty of any wrongdoing in this matter. There is nothing in the judicial system of the United States which ever permits a prosecutor to label as a criminal someone who had not been charged. When the government does charge someone, that person is entitled to a fair hearing to respond to the government's charges; that is the essence of due process. By venturing outside these fundamental boundaries of our legal system, the Independent Counsel has fashioned theories into conclusions which would not have survived an open search for the truth."[152]

- "The Final Report . . . represents an assault on the foundations of Anglo-American jurisprudence. Rather than indicting and bringing to trial those whom he speculates may have acted illegally in connection with the Iran-Contra affair, the Independent Counsel has instead established himself as judge and jury. Having reached private, nonjudicial verdicts of "guilty" concerning those whom he dares not indict, the Independent Counsel seeks now to dispatch his intended victims to the gallows of public condemnation."[153]

- "One of the essential elements of the American legal system, a cardinal rule of every prosecutor, is articulated in an expression well-known to anyone raised in this country: 'Put up of shut up.' The Independent Counsel has done neither."[154]

Former President George Bush

- "The investigation conducted by the Office of Independent Counsel ("OIC") under Judge Lawrence Walsh has largely been an inquiry into a political dispute between a Republican Administration and a Democratic Congress over foreign policy."[155]

- "OIC has spend over six years and $40 million trying to give a criminal hue to the serious constitutional struggle over separation of powers between the Congress and the Executive in the foreign policy area."

- "[T]he real thrust of its conclusions relate to purported contravention of government policy. The Independent Counsel's authorizing legislation did not contemplate the investigation of such policy differences."

- "Congress has used the Independent Counsel criminal statute as a tool for inserting itself into foreign policy, which is reserved under the Constitution to the Executive. An attempt to criminalize public policy differences jeopardizes any President's ability to govern."

- Bush's attorneys (King & Spalding) reviewed 111 boxes of files stored at the National Archives and produced 6,500 pages of unclassified documents related to Iran/Contra and all documents related to Bush's diary.[156]

- OIC originally directed King & Spalding to review 400 boxes of documents stored at the Bush Presidential Materials Project in College Station Texas.

- King & Spalding produced 29,000 pages of documents from President Bush's "chron" files.

- OIC closed its investigation of Bush as "complete" because Bush had made full disclosure. But when Bush pardoned Weinberger, OIC reopened the investigation in order to sabotage the Bush re-election.[157]

Duane Clarridge

- "From my point of view, I certainly hope you will not seal this document for it illustrates, even without my counter arguments, what frivolous, shallowly based indictments Walsh et al brought against me. Thus the motivation of this man Walsh, who is known to be sotted with egotistical greed, must be vengeance -- I would not curtsy to his request to turn state 'snitch' and denied him another undeserved 'scalp' of his tenure."[158]

Thomas Clines

- Clines made a mistake on his 1985 income tax return when he was overworked in securing the release of American hostages and assisting the Contras in forcing the communists to have free elections. He filed an amended and corrected return.

- The OIC later charged him of tax fraud. The jury, confused by the IC's trial tactics, found Clines guilty of under-reporting. The charges against Clines of under-reporting or failing to declare foreign financial accounts were untrue. Clines spent his life's fortune appealing his case to the U.S. Supreme Court. In the meantime he spent a year in jail "because of an overzealous, vindictive Independent Counsel who operated for seven years with no supervision."[159]

- For several pages Clines lists Walsh's false statements about him in the Final Report and provides documentary evidence of the truth.

Edwin G. Corr

- Walsh states that Corr presented false testimony, and that Walsh had sufficient evidence to prosecute him successfully but chose not to do so.[160] Walsh misrepresents the evidence and testimony on the events in question.[161]

- Prior to the publication of the Final Report, Corr had never been a target of the investigation. He had even been informed in 1991 by a letter from the IC that he was not a target.

- By 1991 and 1992 the IC was desperate to get convictions to offset the growing suspicion that he was wasting the taxpayer's money on a witchhunt with no results.

Robert C. Dutton

- "The many instances of misstatement of fact and the use of innuendo cause me to believe that Mr. Walsh is trying to rewrite history to make it fit concepts he was never able to prove in a court of law."[162]

- Secord was not operating under the control of Oliver North.

- The Boland Amendment did not apply to Dutton's activities. "The IC well knows that this amendment applied only to U.S. Government appropriated funds and therefore had no bearing on our activities. This is a prime example of the I.C. ignoring fact in order to taint the activity with illegality."[163]

- North did not direct Secord to purchase an aircraft as IC asserts. Secord had the money and authority to purchase it. North had neither.

- IC falsely asserts North frequently gave Dutton orders. North gave none. Secord gave the orders.

- IC says their operation was unlawful when it was not. It was a legal action secretly undertaken on behalf of and with the support of the U.S. Government.

- "To brand those of us who supported the government as 'outlaws' is slanderous. Unsubstantiated allegations and insinuations such as this should not be allowed to be part of this report."[164]

- Walsh says that Dutton lied to the families or did not care about his people when he did not pay the $60,000 death benefit to the families of the crewmen killed in the Hasenfus shootdown. Walsh himself had stopped the payment by deceiving the Swiss government into freezing the accounts out of which the benefit was to be paid.

- The report repeatedly links North with meetings or other activities where North was not present.

- The report said nothing about Dutton's efforts which led to the release of American hostages.

Lt. Col. Robert Earl, Ret.

- "The inappropriateness of public release of this document is specifically attested to by the damage that would result to at least thirty-one (31) named individuals that would be publicly branded as wrongdoers by virtue of a chapter being dedicated to each of them. (This has the appearance of vindictiveness and revenge – getting back at people that Judge Walsh things 'escaped' punishment.) The OIC report makes allegations that if true should have been prosecuted, and yet were not. If not true, they should not be published to besmirch persons unfairly."[165]

- "The document has an unfair, biased view of events. One interpretation of events is made, viewed from the perspective of the OIC's interpretation that individuals committed crimes. (In our system of justice, a judge and jury make this determination, not an Independent Counsel)."[166]

Joseph F. Fernandez

- The classic scapegoat. As CIA station chief in Costa Rica, he carried out duties assigned from Washington. His superiors denied knowledge of the Nicaraguan operation. Fernandez was interviewed by the Tower Commission in January 1987 and admitted his involvement in peripheral activities related to Nicaragua at precisely the same moment that his superiors were denying any involvement.

- Fernandez cooperated from the beginning until he learned that he would be taking the blame along with Oliver North.

- The evidence was overwhelming that his superiors knew. The IC had that evidence. But when Fernandez realized that he was being thrown overboard, he claimed his Fifth Amendment right. Walsh was furious with Fernandez, and, accusing him of being uncooperative, brought the full weight of the U.S. government against him.

- Fernandez was indicted twice, but both times the cases were dismissed. The dismissals were upheld on appeal. The IC's Final Report concluded anyway that Fernandez violated the Boland Amendments, made false statements, and committed other crimes. The report gives a misleading explanation of why the cases were dismissed.

Norman Gardner

- Gardner was asked to give information to an FBI investigator as a witness. He did so on ten separate occasions and later found that the investigator's notes and written summaries were inaccurate. These notes were used against him by the IC to try to make him fall into the perjury trap, even though the prosecutors already knew that there were dozens of mistakes in the notes and that they were seriously flawed.

- Gardner refused to serve again as a witness for the IC except before a grand jury, under oath, pursuant to a subpoena, his responses being transcribed, and with him being designated in the status of a "witness."

- On those terms, the IC had Gardner testify for 3 1/2 hours before a grand jury. Later, the FBI requested another interview. Gardner said yes, but only on the same conditions. An hour and a half later he was called by phone and told that he was now a "target" of the investigation.

- He was subpoenaed to testify to secret matters, but his lawyer did not yet have a security clearance. While his attorney was going through the requirements of getting the security clearance, Mr. Gardner was taken before the Grand Jury and repeatedly questioned, requiring him to claim his Fifth Amendment privilege. This was the IC's ploy to make him appear unresponsive before the Grand Jury.

- In the Final Report, the IC asserts that he could not get information about some of the very matters of which Gardner had earlier testified under oath or had addressed in many hours of interviews.

- "The questions asked of Mr. Gardner before the grand jury on August 7, 1991, at a time when the Independent Counsel knew that for technical reasons Mr. Gardner was under counsel's instruction to invoke privilege, were designed to create an impression that information was being denied the prosecutors, but the questions were the same ones he had already answered in April. That false impression has now been memorialized in the Independent Counsel's report."[167]

- Numerous other insinuations of criminal wrongdoing are made against Gardner in other parts of the Report. Gardner was never indicted nor tried for any of these supposed crimes.

Response of Clair George

- The Final Report describes Mr. George as being guilty of numerous crimes of which he was acquitted in two jury trials.[168]

- Mr. George says that the OIC intentionally relied on fabricated documents as well as evidence rejected by the Court to reach his conclusions of George's supposed criminal guilt.

- George points out the problems with the accuracy of the grand jury transcripts. Written transcripts of verbal exchanges between attorneys and witnesses during the grand jury are shown to be sometimes in error when compared with sound recordings made of those exchanges. Written transcripts have witnesses answering yes or no to the wrong part of a multiple part answer.

Ambassador Donald P. Gregg

- Mr. Gregg was accused in the Final Report of acts of concealment and "possible false testimony," although no evidence of any kind was ever developed or presented, and Mr. Gregg was never formally charged with any crime. Supposedly, he was guilty of participating in a coverup because he did not immediately and voluntarily go to the news media for a press conference to rebut the White House announcement in October 1986 that the U.S. Government had no connection to the Hasenfus plane which had been shot down.[169]

- Gregg fully cooperated with the Independent Counsel's investigation. He had nothing to hide. That is why he was shocked when he was told that he had failed their lie detector test. An independent expert confirmed that he had not, and that the Independent Counsel's office had misrepresented the results of the test. This way, they could have another victim to prosecute since they were losing Oliver North. To cover their tracks, they gave Gregg a second polygraph test which he passed.

Albert Hakim

- Mr. Hakim is one of the worst victims ever of any official wrong act of the United States government. His contracts were with the State Department, which officially denied any responsibility for his initiatives. His treatment at the hands of the IC and his abandonment by the persons in the Reagan Administration who were responsible for Iran/Contra is unconscionable. His abandonment by his own government is reminiscent of the U.S.'s abandonment of the Viet Nam POWs.

- Hakim asks the same question that I did beginning in December of 1986: why did the

Reagan Administration handle the exposure of the secret operations as if it was the guilty party?[170]

- When those operations "became the focus of public awareness the Reagan administration handled the exposure as if it was a guilty party. It therefore, lost the opportunity to take responsibility for the activities and, as such, to protect their sensitive and proper mission."[171]

- "The activities themselves were not manifestly illegal and were certainly defensible to the American people; had the President decided to stand up for the policy he had initiated and supported. Instead, by acting as if something had been done that was regrettable in a moral, legal or political sense, the president showed a political vulnerability that invited the sharks into the boat. Unfortunately for the participants, the president was far away from the boat when his advisors started the finger pointing process."[172]

- "Throughout the entire process of revelation and investigation, the pressure has been on those participants to 'give up' the President."[173]

- "As the administration distanced itself from the activities of the Iran Contra initiatives, it abandoned people in the United States and around the world who were quietly working to enable the USG interests to be realized."

- "The bulk of these people had been participating solely because the President or his representatives had asked them in the name of the Executive Branch and under the guise of a legal process that insured legality and official endorsement."

- "Once the scrutiny began the participants in the 'field' were not only left without the support that was due them, they became the focus of blame for the activities themselves. This abandonment served the Reagan political needs for distance and had a devastating effect on those left holding the bag" (to the tune of tens of millions of dollars and also lives lost).

- Albert Hakim "was functioning as a private citizen who made a business arrangement with the USG to assist them in a variety of foreign policy objectives."[174]

- "The dynamic between the two major political parties was predictable once Reagan showed weakness rather than strength on this issue. The wild card was the dynamic adopted and created by Independent Counsel Walsh in his investigations."

- "Once the Reagan administration decided to abandon those offering assistance, a variety of things happened. Many people were jailed in the Middle East countries as their role on behalf of the USG became known. In Beirut, alone, over ten people were jailed and were abandoned by the USG." The moderate faction in Iran which had been working with the U.S. government was brought to an abrupt end by the Ayatollah.

- Hakim primarily blames Reagan. But he has this to say about the IC: "The treatment by the USG through the Office of Independent Counsel (OIC) has been marked by changing stories, deceptive evidence gathering, tortious business interference, misrepresentations, attempts to undermine the benefit of the presumption of innocence that Americans enjoy as the hallmark of our democracy, fabrications and a personal twist to prosecution and litigation that even the news media has observed."[175]

- The IC first told the Swiss government to freeze Hakim's international business accounts because they were an illegal international rogue operation. Upon investigation, the Swiss government decided to unfreeze the accounts, to which the IC said that Hakim was an official government agent who had yet to make an "accounting" to the U.S. Government.

- Hakim says that the IC created a false scenario illegally to deceive the Swiss government to hand over Swiss banking documents, which it used out of context, to attempt to bring criminal convictions in American Courts. He alleges that the defendants were unable to get companion documents from the Swiss government due to bank secrecy laws, meanwhile the IC's copies of those exculpatory documents had been held back or destroyed.

Former Attorney General Edwin Meese III

- "Walsh has carried on a six-and-a-half year fruitless search for nonexistent criminal offenses and substituted politically-oriented hostility for objective fact-finding. In the process Walsh has violated numerous laws, professional standards, and ethical requirement. The true total cost of this malfeasance approximates $100,000,000." [176]

- "To avoid the public criticism official condemnation, and punitive action his conduct deserves, Walsh is using his final Report (as he did his Fourth Interim Report to Congress) to divert attention from his own failures and misconduct by falsely accusing President Reagan and his top officials of fictional offenses wholly manufactured by Walsh."[177]

- "Walsh's Report is . . . an unconscionable act of deception intended to coverup Walsh's own unethical and illegal conduct, divert attention from Walsh's years of prosecutorial incompetence and abuse, and smear the Reagan Administration. . . ."[178]

- "Walsh's . . . despicable manipulation and omission of information – would be laughable if it were not so deplorable. . . . This report conceals obvious and important facts that give the lie to Walsh's bizarre conspiracy fiction."[179]

- Walsh's Report violates special investigation and prosecution standards laid down by the Watergate Special Prosecution Force.[180]

- The Report contains alleged facts about alleged criminal activities which were not previously disclosed in a public forum.

- The Report makes accusations of criminality toward persons who were not charged with criminal misconduct after being thoroughly and exhaustively investigated.

- Even though Meese appointed Walsh as a justice department official when questions were raised about the constitutionality of the independent counsel law, Walsh denied every request by Meese for access to the information which Walsh claimed as the basis for his allegations.

- Walsh purported the myth that the Attorney General believed the HAWK shipment was illegal. Meese provides documentation to show that such was not the case.

- Meese explains, contrary to Walsh's seven year insistence, that the November HAWK shipment was legal.[181] Walsh never prosecuted a single official for violating any law related to the shipment, yet always maintained its illegality as the starting point for his persecutorial campaign.

- Walsh brought indictments against North (Counts 7 and 8) and others for obstructing an investigation by Meese between November 21 - 24, 1986, which Meese says never took place! Meese at first undertook an informal fact-finding inquiry which later led to an investigation. But at the time, no investigation was underway. It was not a criminal investigation.[182] The Attorney General said repeatedly in public that this was not an investigation!

- In contrast to the restrained and even-handed conduct of the Watergate Task Force, "Walsh's Report is 'irresponsible and unethical.' Walsh takes a sledgehammer to over 200 years of American jurisprudence and his misconduct evidences an out-of-control prosecutor unable and unwilling to abide by the rule of law."[183]

- Walsh overcharged the government by $78,000 for meals and hotel expenses.[184]

- Walsh used a government-leased vehicle for traveling between his office and his Watergate hotel suite, when the expense was not supposed to be allowed.[185]

- He traveled first class by air for two years without being properly certified or authorized as required, and allowed 30 members of his staff to accrue excess leave without written justification or approval, amounting to some 5,300 hours by March 31, 1992.[186]

- The rules required him to reimburse the taxpayers for these staff costs, but Congress waived the requirement at Walsh's request. It is clear for whom he was working and what the rewards were.[187]

- Rather than being penalized or punished for clear violations of federal laws and regulations, or being forced to repay the taxpayers by repaying the treasury, Walsh was allowed by Congress to have the taxpayers foot the bill.

- Walsh received numerous unallowable payments while prosecuting others for conspiracy to defraud the United States.[188]

- On at least two occasions, Walsh violated U.S. laws regulating the use and possession of classified documents and information.

- Walsh read highly classified information while flying on a commercial airplane. A government contractor observed the violation and reported him to the FBI. Walsh was neither reprimanded nor punished.[189]

- Walsh negligently lost a suitcase full of classified documents when he checked them *at curbside* as luggage at Los Angeles International Airport! These highly classified government documents included secret codes! Walsh kept the loss secret for more than two weeks before notifying the justice department.

- "Walsh's treatment of highly classified material – entrusted to him by the government – and his violations of security rules known to him, shows extraordinary arrogance, contempt for the law, and bad judgment. . . . Unlike most citizens, who would be punished for such misconduct, Walsh escaped even a mild reprimand."[190]

- Neither Meese, nor anyone else mentioned in Walsh's report, was allowed to read the full report until after it was punished. Those who were accused were given only the highly edited excerpts that Walsh wanted them to read. Therefore, no single individual had an opportunity to learn except in a very truncated way, the accusations to which they were responding.

- Walsh repeatedly used or alluded to secret grand jury testimony in his Final Report, which is improper and violates the Federal Rules of Criminal Procedure.[191]

- Walsh discusses the grand jury testimony of persons like Meese who, because of Grand Jury secrecy rules, can never have access to that same testimony to see if Walsh has cited it correctly.

- "With the degree of fairness accorded by prosecutors during the Salem witch trials, Walsh obstructed virtually every effort by the Attorney General to review the information allegedly gathered by Walsh to manufacture his inane conspiracy and coverup theory."[192]

- "Walsh demands that those he accuses (as well as the public) be satisfied with his self-serving and tortured representations and characterizations of information, and willingly accept the guilty verdict he imposes on them."[193]

- "Walsh's Report is thoroughly defective, and his conduct is dishonest and cowardly. Walsh's malfeasance and abuse of power are unequaled in recent American history and pose a real and serious danger to our system of justice."

- "Furthermore, the severe damage Walsh attempts to inflict on innocent people – under the guise of justice – is intended to have a devastating and lasting impact on their lives. For this he must be viewed with contempt. History will judge Walsh harshly, and well it should."[194]

Ronald Reagan

- "The Iran-Contra Independent Counsel has misused and abused the reporting process that is mandated by the independent counsel statute. The Final Report unfairly and unnecessarily injures the rights and reputations of individuals, relies on innuendo, speculation and conjecture instead of proof, violates established standards governing the conduct of prosecutors, and improperly relies on secret grand jury materials to support the Independent Counsel's many accusations."[195]

- "[T]he evidence is overwhelming that the essential facts of the Iranian initiative were readily and repeatedly disclosed by President Reagan and his top advisers. . . . In fact, President Reagan's knowledge of the 1985 arms transactions supports, not undermines, the legality of those transactions."[196]

- No civil laws were violated by the Iranian arms shipments. There is strong authority for the President's actions.[197]

- The Boland Amendment was not violated.[198]

- Walsh failed to comply with Department of Justice rules, regulations, and ethical provisions when determining the content of his Final Report.[199] 28 U.S.C. Section 594(f) requires the independent counsel to comply with written or other established policies of the Department of Justice. Walsh refused to comply.

- Walsh violated ordinary ethical standards imposed on prosecutors generally.[200]

- Federal Courts have ruled repeatedly to protect grand jury secrecy and to prohibit the public use of grand jury testimony.[201]

- Walsh improperly relied on Grand Jury materials, including "double-hearsay." There are at least 648 specific references of one kind or another to secret grand jury testimony or exhibits from 62 different witnesses in Volume 1 of the Final Report. This is an average of more than one instance per page.

- "Indeed the filing of final reports by independent counsels based upon grand jury material 'is contrary to the practice of federal grand jury investigations,'. . . and seriously undermines the constitutional guarantee of grand jury secrecy."[202]

- Walsh made repeated improper public disclosures, both with his public interim reports and with his statements to the media and television appearances.[203]

Maj. Gen. Richard V. Secord, USAF Ret.

- "On Sept. 7, 1993 I petitioned the court for permission to read the entire report, but the request was denied by order of November 22, 1993. This denial vitiates the intentions of Congress, and I find myself forced to rebut fragments of what purports to be a comprehensive story."[204]

- "I append to this letter a litany of distortions, false official statements, fabrications and outright lies perpetrated by the IC."[205]

- "I knew Lawrence Walsh to be a liar when he testified before Judge Gesell in a Kastigar hearing in June 1988. Two months before this hearing Walsh told me (in the presence of witnesses) that he '...had watched my testimony in Congress and was very impressed.' When I started expressing amazement and when his aides gave him sharp looks he said, 'Except when you talked about the money.' This of course was a joke since Albert Hakim's ledgers (secured through a grant of immunity) were the focus of the entire hearing. Incredibly, Walsh denied, under oath, having seen any of this. He took this position to avoid being 'tainted' and losing his indictment. He is a liar!"[206]

EPILOGUE

North and the South

Uncle Ollie's Cabin

I said at the beginning that this book was not written simply to help win an election. If my goal had been only to further the candidacy of Oliver North, I would have written a much different book with a less obscure title. Whether Colonel North wins or loses in the November 1994 election is not the issue.

The issue is what kind of government we will have under our Constitution and whether the rights guaranteed by the Constitution will remain secure. One of those is the right not to be attainted by the Congress of the United States. In the end, Oliver North is a citizen. If the Constitution cannot protect him when the government acts to take away his rights, will it protect you or me?

On the political level, it is important for voters to be able to make an informed choice based on the whole truth. At the present time many people in the Commonwealth of Virginia have a negative view of Oliver North based on misinformation because of his political branding.

Through this book I have tried to expose the political ruse that was perpetrated by Congress and by certain politically powerful people in the summer of 1987. In this case, the truth helps Oliver North. I hope that my fellow Virginians will read the book and be helped by it, and then vote whichever way they choose.

I have tried simply to present the truth as best as I am able to understand it. Mistakes are inevitable. This book is certain to have its share of them. The Iran/Contra depositions alone take up 27 volumes and more than 30,000 pages. The transcripts of the hearings take up many more thousands of pages, as do the declassified documents and exhibits. It has not been possible for me to study every fragment of public data or testimony.

Doubtless, there are Washington insiders who know many intimate and secret details which I do not and who have a better grasp of the facts and data than I do. I expect to hear from them and possibly to be severely criticized by some of them on matters for which I may have been mistaken. But my research since the summer of 1987 has not changed the perspective I had as early as January 1987. If anything, my study of the data has made me more convinced than ever of the innocence of Oliver North, and that he was treated shamefully by his own government in violation of the U.S. Constitution.

Let me make quite clear what I am not saying since there will be those who jump to unwarranted conclusions by what I have written. First, I am not saying that Congress is without any authority over foreign policy. I am not arguing for an imperial presidency. Congress's power over foreign policy rivals the President's and both branches should work in concert toward a unified foreign policy. The point of my protest in this book is simply to insist that Congress cannot through legislation take away the foreign policy powers vested in the President by the Constitution. The President's foreign policy powers remain potent even if Congress by law tries to diminish them.

Second, by criticizing Congress for trying to make policy differences criminal, I am not thereby arguing for or against the merits of the Iran initiative or the merits of the Nicaraguan initiative. Whether the missile transfers to Iran were prudent is a matter on which fair minded people may legitimately disagree. And the support or nonsupport of the Contras is a matter on which fair minded people may legitimately disagree. Not all republicans supported President Reagan in those policies, and not all democrats disagreed with him.

The point here is no different than to say that Jimmy Carter as president had the authority to have a foreign policy based on human rights, for example, rather than on economic detente. It was not for Congress to dictate what kind of foreign policy President Reagan sought to implement any more than to dictate the foreign policy rationale of Presidents Carter or Ford. The wisdom and effectiveness of their foreign policies is an entirely different question than whether they had the authority to conceive and implement such policies in the first place.

Some conservative supporters of Oliver North may wish that this book did not see the light of day, to keep some of the old issues from being rehashed. Other conservatives may fear that my arguments will condemn them also because conservatives have at times been guilty of holding politically motivated hearings (e.g., the McCarthy hearings). My answer is that I do not care whether it is liberals or conservatives who are violating the Constitution by holding political trials, both are wrong to do so. If conservatives are embarrassed, so be it.

Others may dispute my approach to separation of powers in my comments about the President's relation to Congress's laws and the Supreme Court's opinions. My views are not radical. I suggest, for example, that my critics read the first and second inaugural addresses of Abraham Lincoln, the Federalist Papers, and the opinions of Chief Justice John Marshall. My views derive from such sources as these and are not outside the pale of our country's traditions.

Some may believe that I have a disdain for Congress. No. I have a disdain for politicians who use the political machinery of Congress to violate the Constitution of the United States and the rights of American citizens. When elected members act in the name of Congress, or by or on behalf of Congress, as agents of the majority their acts are the acts of Congress. In such a case, it is right to criticize "Congress" even though individual members may themselves dissent from the official misconduct perpetrated by the majority.

Regardless of what Oliver North's political fortunes

turn out to be, in 1987 he was abused by the Congress of the United States which denied him his rights under the Constitution and unlawfully attainted him in an effort to destroy his reputation and his future. That was wrong. It could have been either you or me.

I am convinced that Oliver North served the United States with honor, vigor, and selflessness. He has my full respect and complete trust. As a professional military officer he followed what he believed to be lawful orders from the highest executive official in our government. When those above him felt that they could not take the political responsibility for their own policies, he sought to protect his commander in chief by accepting political blame. But he did not bargain for charges of criminality which arose when Congress tried to make policy differences a crime.

One can only speculate whether the former President believed that it was better for a subordinate to be expended rather than to confront Congress directly on sharply divisive disputes over policy. It is tempting, in light of the mountains of data, to believe that North was made the scapegoat for policies over which the former president was unwilling to battle with Congress.

Those policies were at worst embarrassing only, and not criminal. Therefore I have yet to understand why the former President refused to take responsibility for his own policies or to put a stop to the prosecutorial bloodletting of his subordinates in the executive branch. However, the Appeals Court has since spoken, and now it is time for Colonel North to get his reputation back, and to receive the honor due him.

APPENDIX A

January 17, 1986 Presidential Finding Authorizing the Iranian Initiative

The following eleven pages contain reproductions of the declassified January 17, 1986 Covert Action Memo on Iran to President Reagan, and the accompanying Covert Action Finding.

Note the President's initials approving the three-page Memo and his signature approving the one-page Finding. Of interest is the fact that the policy memo was prepared by Oliver North. The Memo was presented to President Reagan by John Poindexter, the President's National Security Advisor.

Also of interest is the handwritten notation at the bottom of page three which reads: "President was briefed verbally from this paper. VP, Don Regan and Don Fortier were present."

For the reader's convenience, a typewritten reproduction of the Memo and the Finding is also included.

THE WHITE HOUSE

WASHINGTON

January 17, 1986

ACTION

MEMORANDUM FOR THE PRESIDENT

FROM: JOHN M. POINDEXTER

SUBJECT: Covert Action Finding Regarding Iran

Prime Minister Peres of Israel secretly dispatched his special advisor on terrorism with instructions to propose a plan by which Israel, with limited assistance from the U.S., can create conditions to help bring about a more moderate government in Iran. The Israelis are very concerned that Iran's deteriorating position in the war with Iraq, the potential for further radicalization in Iran, and the possibility of enhanced Soviet influence in the Gulf all pose significant threats to the security of Israel. They believe it is essential that they act to at least preserve a balance of power in the region.

The Israeli plan is premised on the assumption that moderate elements in Iran can come to power if these factions demonstrate their credibility in defending Iran against Iraq and in deterring Soviet intervention. To achieve the strategic goal of a more moderate Iranian government, the Israelis are prepared to unilaterally commence selling military material to Western-oriented Iranian factions. It is their belief that by so doing they can achieve a heretofore unobtainable penetration of the Iranian governing hierarchy. The Israelis are convinced that the Iranians are so desperate for military materiel, expertise and intelligence that the provision of these resources will result in favorable long-term changes in personnel and attitudes within the Iranian government. Further, once the exchange relationship has commenced, a dependency would be established on those who are providing the requisite resources, thus allowing the provider(s) to coercively influence near-term events. Such an outcome is consistent with our policy objectives and would present significant advantages for U.S. national interests. As described by the Prime Minister's emissary, the only requirement the Israelis have is an assurance that they will be allowed to purchase U.S. replenishments for the stocks that they sell to Iran. We have researched the legal problems of Israel's selling U.S. manufactured arms to Iran. Because of the requirement in U.S. law for recipients of U.S. arms to notify the U.S. government of transfers to third countries, I do not recommend that you agree with the specific details of the Israeli plan. However, there is another possibility. Some time ago Attorney

General William French Smith determined that under an appropriate finding you could authorize the CIA to sell arms to countries outside of the provisions of the laws and reporting requirements for foreign military sales. The objectives of the Israeli plan could be met if the CIA, using an authorized agent as necessary, purchased arms from the Department of Defense under the Economy Act and then transferred them to Iran directly after receiving appropriate payment from Iran.

The Covert Action Finding attached at Tab A provides the latitude for the transactions indicated above to proceed. The Iranians have indicated an immediate requirement for 4,000 basic TOW weapons for use in the launchers they already hold.

The Israeli's are also sensitive to a strong U.S. desire to free our Beirut hostages and have insisted that the Iranians demonstrate both influence and good intent by an early release of the five Americans. Both sides have agreed that the hostages will be immediately released upon commencement of this action. Prime Minister Peres had his emissary pointedly note that they well understand our position on not making concessions to terrorists. They also point out, however, that terrorist groups, movements, and organizations are significantly easier to influence through governments than they are by direct approach. In that we have been unable to exercise any suasion over Hizballah during the course of nearly two years of kidnappings, this approach through the government of Iran may well be our only way to achieve the release of the Americans held in Beirut. It must again be noted that since this dialogue with the Iranians began in September, Reverend Weir has been released and there have been no Shia terrorist attacks against American or Israeli persons, property, or interests.

Therefore it is proposed that Israel make the necessary arrangements for the sale of 4000 TOW weapons to Iran. Sufficient funds to cover the sale would be transferred to an agent of the CIA. The CIA would then purchase the weapons from the Department of Defense and deliver the weapons to Iran through the agent. If all of the hostages are not released after the first shipment of 1000 weapons, further transfers would cease.

On the other hand, since hostage release is in some respects a byproduct of a larger effort to develop ties to potentially moderate forces in Iran, you may wish to redirect such transfers to other groups within the government at a later time.

The Israelis have asked for our urgent response to this proposal so that they can plan accordingly. They note that conditions inside both Iran and Lebanon are highly volatile. The Israelis are cognizant that this entire operation will be terminated if the Iranians abandon their goal of moderating their government or allow further acts of terrorism. You have discussed the general outlines of the Israeli plan with Secretaries Shultz and Weinberger, Attorney General Meese and Director Casey. The Secretaries do not recommend you proceed with this plan. Attorney General Meese and Director Casey believe the short-term and long-term objectives of the plan warrant the policy risks involved and recommend you approve the attached Finding. Because of the extreme sensitivity of this project, it is recommended that you exercise your statutory prerogative to withhold notification of the Finding to the Congressional oversight committees until such time that you deem it to be appropriate.

Recommendation

OK No

RR jr ___ That you sign the attached Finding.

JP

Prepared by:
Oliver L. North

1030 17 Jan 86

Attachment
Tab A - Covert Action Finding

President was briefed verbally from this paper. VP, Don Regan and Don Fortier were present.

JP

Finding Pursuant to Section 662 of The Foreign Assistance Act of 1961 As Amended, Concerning Operations Undertaken by the Central Intelligence Agency in Foreign Countries, Other Than Those Intended Solely for the Purpose of Intelligence Collection

I hereby find that the following operation in a foreign country (including all support necessary to such operation) is important to the national security of the United States, and due to its extreme sensitivity and security risks, I determine it is essential to limit prior notice, and direct the Director of Central Intelligence to refrain from reporting this Finding to the Congress as provided in Section 501 of the National Security Act of 1947, as amended, until I otherwise direct.

SCOPE	DESCRIPTION
Iran	Assist selected friendly foreign liaison services, third countries and third parties which have established relationships with Iranian elements, groups, and individuals sympathetic to U.S. Government interests and which do not conduct or support terrorist actions directed against U.S. persons, property or interests, for the purpose of: (1) establishing a more moderate government in Iran, (2) obtaining from them significant intelligence not otherwise obtainable, to determine the current Iranian Government's intentions with respect to its neighbors and with respect to terrorist acts, and (3) furthering the release of the American hostages held in Beirut and preventing additional terrorist acts by these groups. Provide funds, intelligence, counter-intelligence, training, guidance and communications and other necessary assistance to these elements, groups, individuals, liaison services and third countries in support of these activities.
	The USG will act to facilitate efforts by third parties and third countries to establish contact with moderate elements within and outside the Government of Iran by providing these elements with arms, equipment and related material in order to enhance the credibility of these elements in their effort to achieve a more pro-U.S. government in Iran by demonstrating their ability to obtain requisite resources to defend their country against Iraq and intervention by the Soviet Union. This support will be discontinued if the U.S. Government learns that these elements have abandoned their goals of moderating their government and appropriated the material for purposes other than that provided by this Finding.

Ronald Reagan

The White House
Washington, D.C.
Date January 17, 1986

of the extreme sensitivity of this project, it is recommended that you exercise your statutory prerogative to withhold notification of the Finding to the Congressional oversight committees until such time that you deem it to be appropriate.

<u>Recommendation</u>

OK	NO	
RR	___	That you sign the attached Finding.

Prepared by:
Oliver L. North

Attachment
Tab A - Covert Action Finding

Recommendation

OK	NO	
RR	___	That you sign the attached Finding.

JP

Prepared by:
Oliver L. North

Attachment
Tab A - Covert Action Finding

1100 17 Jan 86.

President was briefed verbally from this paper. VP, Don Regan and Don Fortier were present.

JP

these activities.

The USG will act to facilitate efforts by third parties and third countries to establish contact with moderate elements within and outside the Government of Iran by providing these elements with arms, equipment and related material in order to enhance the credibility of these elements in their effort to achieve a more pro-U.S. government in Iran by demonstrating their ability to obtain requisite resources to defend their country against Iraq and intervention by the Soviet Union. This support will be discontinued if the U.S. Government learns that these elements have abandoned their goals of moderating their government and appropriated the material for purposes other than that provided by this Finding.

The White House
Washington, D.C.
Date January 17, 1986

THE WHITE HOUSE

WASHINGTON

January 17, 1986

ACTION

MEMORANDUM FOR THE PRESIDENT

FROM: JOHN M. POINDEXTER

SUBJECT: Covert Action Finding Regarding Iran

Prime Minister Peres of Israel secretly dispatched his special advisor on terrorism with instructions to propose a plan by which Israel, with limited assistance from the U.S., can create conditions to help bring about a more moderate government in Iran. The Israelis are very concerned that Iran's deteriorating position in the war with Iraq, the potential for further radicalization in Iran, and the possibility of enhanced Soviet influence in the Gulf all pose significant threats to the security of Israel. They believe it is essential that they act to at least preserve a balance of power in the region.

The Israeli plan is premised on the assumption that moderate elements in Iran can come to power if these factions demonstrate their credibility in defending Iran against Iraq and in deterring Soviet intervention. To achieve the strategic goal of a more moderate Iranian government, the Israelis are prepared to unilaterally commence selling military material to Western-oriented Iranian factions. It is their belief that by so doing they can achieve a heretofore unobtainable penetration of the Iranian governing hierarchy. The Israelis are convinced that the Iranians are so desperate for military materiel, expertise and intelligence that the provision of these resources will result in favorable long-term changes in personnel and attitudes within the Iranian government. Further, once the exchange relationship has commenced, a dependency would be established on those who are providing the requisite resources, thus allowing the provider(s) to coercively influence near-term events. Such an outcome is consistent with our policy objectives and would present significant advantages for U.S. national interests. As described by the Prime Minister's emissary, the only requirement the Israelis have is an assurance that they will be allowed to purchase U.S. replenishments for the stocks that they sell to Iran. We have researched the legal problems of Israel's selling U.S. manufactured arms to Iran. Because of the requirement in U.S. law for recipients of U.S. arms to notify the U.S. government of transfers to third countries, I do not recommend that you agree with the specific details of the Israeli plan. However, there is another possibility. Some time ago Attorney

General William French Smith determined that under an appropriate finding you could authorize the CIA to sell arms to countries outside of the provisions of the laws and reporting requirements for foreign military sales. The objectives of the Israeli plan could be met if the CIA, using an authorized agent as necessary, purchased arms from the Department of Defense under the Economy Act and then transferred them to Iran directly after receiving appropriate payment from Iran.

The Covert Action Finding attached at Tab A provides the latitude for the transactions indicated above to proceed. The Iranians have indicated an immediate requirement for 4,000 basic TOW weapons for use in the launchers they already hold.

The Israeli's are also sensitive to a strong U.S. desire to free our Beirut hostages and have insisted that the Iranians demonstrate both influence and good intent by an early release of the five Americans. Both sides have agreed that the hostages will be immediately released upon commencement of this action. Prime Minister Peres had his emissary pointedly note that they well understand our position on not making concessions to terrorists. They also point out, however, that terrorist groups, movements, and organizations are significantly easier to influence through governments then they are by direct approach, in that we have been unable to exercise any suasion over Hiszballah during the course of nearly two years of kidnappings, this approach through the government of Iran may well by our <u>only</u> way to achieve the release of the Americans held in Beirut. It must be noted that since this dialog with the Iranians began in September, Reverend Weir has been released and there have been no Shia terrorist attacks against American or Israeli persons, property, or interests.

Therefore it is proposed that Israel make the necessary arrangements for the sale of 4000 TOW weapons to Iran. Sufficient funds to cover the sale would be transferred to an agent of the CIA. The CIA would then purchase the weapons from the Department of Defense and deliver the weapons to Iran through the agent. If all of the hostages are not released after the first shipment of 1000 weapons, further transfers would cease.

On the other hand, since hostage release is in some respects a byproduct of a larger effort to develop ties to potentially moderate forces in Iran, you may wish to redirect such transfers to other groups within the government at a later time.

The Israelis have asked for our urgent response to this proposal so that they can plan accordingly. They note that conditions inside both Iran and Lebanon are highly volatile. The Israelis are cognizant that this entire operation will be terminated if the Iranians abandon their goal of moderating their government or allow further acts of terrorism. You have discussed the general outlines of the Israeli plan with Secretaries Shultz and Weinberger, Attorney General Meese and Director Casey. The Secretaries do not recommend you proceed with this plan. Attorney General Meese and Director Casey believe the short-term and long-term objectives of the plan warrant the policy risks involved and recommend you approve the attached finding. Because of the extreme sensitivity of this project, it is recommended that you exercise your statutory prerogative to withhold notification of the Finding to the Congressional oversight committees until such time that you deem it to be appropriate.

Recommendation

OK NO

__ __ That you sign the attached Finding.

Prepared by:
Oliver L. North

Attachment

Tab A - Covert Action Finding

Finding Pursuant to Section 662 of The Foreign Assistance Act of 1961 As Amended, Concerning Operations Undertaken in Foreign Countries, Other Than Those Intended Solely for the Purpose of Intelligence Collection

I hereby find that the following operation in a foreign country (including all support necessary to such operation) is important to the national security of the United States, and due to its extreme sensitivity and security risks, I determine it is essential to limit prior notice, and direct the Director of Central Intelligence to refrain from reporting this finding to the Congress as provided in Section 501 of the National Security Act of 1947, as amended, until I otherwise direct.

SCOPE	DESCRIPTION
Iran	Assist selected friendly foreign liaison services, third countries and third parties which have established relationships with Iranian elements, groups, and individuals sympathetic to U.S. Government interests and which do not conduct or support terrorist actions directed against U.S. persons, property or interests, for the purpose of: (1) establishing a more moderate government in Iran, (2) obtaining from them significant intelligence not otherwise obtainable, to determine the current Iranian Government's intentions with respect to its neighbors and with respect to terrorist acts, and (3) furthering the release of the American hostages held in Beirut and preventing additional terrorist acts by these groups. Provide funds, intelligence, counter-intelligence, training, guidance and communications and other necessary assistance to these elements, groups, individuals, and liaison services and third countries in support of these activities.
	The USG will act to facilitate efforts by third parties and third countries to establish contact with moderate elements within and outside the Government of Iran by providing these elements with arms, equipment and related material in order to enhance the credibility of these elements in their efforts to achieve a more pro-U.S. government in Iran by demonstrating their ability to obtain requisite resources to defend their country against Iraq and intervention by the Soviet Union. This support will be discontinued if the U.S. Government learns that these elements have abandoned their goals of moderating their government and appropriated the material for purposes other than that provided by this Finding

The White House
Washington, D.C.
Date Jaunary 17, 1986

APPENDIX B

Review of Attainder Law
Summary of Principles

A good starting point for gaining an understanding of bills of attainder is the 1946 Supreme Court case known as U.S. v Lovett. It is found at 328 U.S. 303, 90 L.Ed 1252 (June 3, 1946). There are interesting parallels between the background events of the Lovett case and the situation faced by Oliver North in 1987.

The facts are these. In 1943, at the height of America's preparation for all out war with Nazi Germany, three government employees, Lovett, Watson, and Dodd were singled out by Congress as threats because of their influence in the government. Congress held hearings in which the men were vilified. Then Congress took steps to have them fired.

The three men worked in the executive branch under President Franklin D. Roosevelt. Whether they were to be hired or fired was within the President's prerogative. But Congress passed a law requiring their dismissal. The ostensible reason for the firing was that the three men were "subversives," namely, communist sympathizers. The effect, however, was to exalt the Congress over the executive branch and to put FDR in his place.

To trump the president, Congress placed the requirement as an amendment on an emergency spending bill, the Urgent Deficiency Appropriation Act of 1943. The amendment prohibited any branch of government from paying salaries to the three unless the president himself directly appointed them. To do so would give FDR the appearance of aligning himself with suspected communists and thereby weaken his ability to lead.

If the president signed the bill, he would tacitly admit Congress's right to control the hiring policies of the executive branch. If he did not sign the bill, he would not have the necessary money to carry on the war effort.

FDR signed the bill out of necessity, but under protest. He did not reappoint the three men, nevertheless the executive branch agencies kept them working after the cut-off date set in the legislation. Lovett, Watson, and Dodd sued in federal court to be paid for work done after the cut-off date.

They argued that the law (1) usurped the President's right to control the hiring policies of the executive branch, (2) operated as a bill of attainder, and (3) deprived them of due process. The justice department sided with the three men.

The lawyer for Congress argued that the law was nothing more than an exercise by Congress of its power of the purse since according the Constitution: "No money shall be drawn from the Treasury, but in Consequence of Appropriations made by law." Supposedly, it was simply an exercise of Congress's plenary power over appropriations which is not subject to judicial review.

On appeal, the matter boiled down to whether this law operated as a bill of attainder. The Supreme Court said that it did.

The Political Trial

Lovett, Watson, and Dodd were hailed before the Committee on Un-American Activities headed by Martin Dies. For five years the committee had been compiling lists of "subversives." Congress had already put several laws on the books forbidding anyone to hold a federal job if he had been a member of a political party or organization that advocated the overthrow of the constitutional form of government of the United States. To violate the act was a crime.

At the instigation of Congress, the FBI conducted wholesale investigations of all federal employees. Then, on February 1, 1943, Congressman Dies made a speech naming 39 employees, including Lovett, Watson, and Dodd as "affiliates of communist front organizations."

He declared that they were unfit to hold a government position and urged Congress not to appropriate money for their salaries. Even if Dies was right, this was not a constitutional way to go about solving the problem.

The proposed amendment, naming the three men, was debated for days. Some legislators were satisfied as to the men's "guilt" because Dies's word was enough. Others objected that a "legislative lynching" was taking place resembling the procedures used in the "French Chamber of Deputies during the Reign of Terror." To resolve the question, Congress decided to investigate and hold hearings. The defendants were to be given a chance to "prove themselves innocent" of communism or disloyalty.

The Select Committee

Congress passed a resolution forming a select committee. The committee was given plenary powers, including the ability (1) to accuse witnesses of crimes so that the witness would have the burden of proving his own innocence, (2) to subpoena witnesses and papers, (3) to cause witnesses to testify without full representation by a lawyer, and (4) to report its findings and conclusions to the House.

The three accused men were found to be unfit to hold a position of trust with the government.

After days of bitter debate, the amendment (called Section 304) was passed, but the committee report was not attached to it. Upon signing the bill, President Roosevelt said of the amendment, "I have been forced to yield, to avoid delaying our conduct of the war. But I cannot so yield without placing on the record my view that this provision is not only unwise and discriminatory, but unconstitutional."

The Supreme Court's Opinion

The Court found that Congress's purpose was not merely to cut off the disbursement of funds to the Lovett, Watson, and Dodd, but "permanently to bar them from government service."

> What is involved here is a Congressional proscription of Lovett, Watson, and Dodd, prohibiting their ever holding a Government job. Were this case to be not justiciable, Congressional action aimed at three named

> individuals, which stigmatized their reputation and seriously impaired their chance to earn a living, could never be challenged in any court. Our Constitution did not contemplate such a result
>
> We hold that § 304 falls precisely within the category of Congressional actions which the Constitution barred by providing that "No Bill of Attainder . . . shall be passed." A bill of attainder is a legislative Act which inflicts punishment without a judicial trial.[207]

After reviewing previous Supreme Court cases dealing with bills of attainder the Court pointed out that

> They stand for the proposition that legislative acts, no matter what their form, that apply either to named individuals or to easily ascertainable members of a group in such a way as to inflict punishment on them without a judicial trial are bills of attainder prohibited by the constitution.[208]

In discussing what some of those forms might be, the Court included (1) punishing someone by permanently proscribing him from any opportunity to serve the government, and (2) stating that someone is "odious" and guilty of dangerous crimes such as treason, acceptance of bribes, or disloyalty to the country or the constitution. In this case, "permanent proscription from any opportunity to serve the Government is punishment, and of a most severe type."[209]

Congress had tried to inflict a punishment on Lovett, Watson, and Dodd which had not been determined by a previous law or fixed rule, and without giving them the safeguards of a judicial trial. To this the Court replied, "The Constitution declares that that cannot be done either by a state or by the United States."[210]

> Those who wrote our Constitution well knew the danger inherent in special legislative acts which take away life, liberty, or property of particular named persons, because the legislature thinks them guilty of conduct which deserves punishment. They intended to safeguard the people of this country from punishment without trial by duly constituted courts. . . . And even the courts to which this important function was entrusted, were commanded to stay their hands until and unless certain tested safeguards were observed. An accused in court must be tried by an impartial jury, has a right to be represented by counsel, he must be clearly informed of the charge against him . . . he must be confronted by the witnesses against him, he must not be compelled to incriminate himself, . . .[211]

The Court concluded by saying that "When our Constitution and Bill of Rights were written, our ancestors had ample reason to know that legislative trials and punishments were too dangerous to liberty to exist in the nation of free men they envisioned. And so they proscribed bills of attainder."[212]

A Matter of Definition

The test for a bill of attainder, the Court said, is whether an act of Congress accomplishes punishment of a named individual without a judicial trial. In the Lovett case, the act naming the three individuals was passed at the end of the legislative trial and was signed into law.

The Court defined punishment as being any result where life, liberty, or property is taken from a named person whom Congress thinks is guilty of conduct which deserves punishment. The amount of punishment is immaterial, so long as punishment in some form is inflicted. Punishment clearly takes place when some form of retribution is exacted.

Harm is not necessarily punishment. Some right to life, liberty, or property must have been infringed. For example, the deprivation of any civil right would qualify as punishment.

When we apply these principles to Oliver North's situation we find that he had everyman's right to an unbiased grand jury. The Appeals Court held that Congress and the Independent Counsel had tainted both the grand jury and the trial jury. North's civil right was thus deprived, meeting the definition of punishment in the U.S. v Lovett case. This was only one form of punishment meted out to him by Congress.

In America, each citizen has a property right in his own reputation and character. That is why our laws prohibit slander and libel. If the effect of Congress's action is to stigmatize the accused, as happened to Oliver North in 1987, punishment has been inflicted by abridging his property right in his reputation.

In the Lovett case, Section 304 itself never specified an offense and did not directly allege guilt. That would have been so clumsy on the part of Congress that no one would have been fooled by it. Rather, Section 304 was written dryly and innocuously to disguise the unconstitutional setting of the accompanying political trial and to make a way for Congress to deny that it had slandered the three accused men. Section 304 did not have the obvious appearance of a bill of attainder. The bare text of the law itself simply ended the paychecks of three named persons.

But there had been (1) a bill naming individuals, (2) a legislative trial, before and during which pronouncements of guilt were made, and (3) conclusions of guilt which were published in the committee report to Congress. Thus, the elements of a bill of attainder had been met. In Lovett, Watson, and Dodd's situation a law had been passed at the end of the process as well.

By comparison, in March 1987 federal rules were published naming Oliver North as the object of the Independent Counsel's investigation.[213] In July 1987 Congress held a legislative trial, before and during which various legislators made pronouncements of North's guilt. Conclusions about his guilt were published on numerous occasions by Congress and on behalf of Congress by Lawrence Walsh. Therefore, the elements of a bill of attainder were met.

Is This a Bill?

Article 1, Section 9, Clause 3 mandates that "No Bill of Attainder or ex post facto law shall be passed." These two clauses immediately point out the contrast between bills and laws. Not all bills become laws.

The Constitution does not use the words "law of attainder," it uses the words "bill of attainder." A "bill" does not have to be enacted as legislation to be a "bill" of attainder. It is enough that the bill exists as a resolution passed by Congress or some similar "bill" that is passed and whose contents are disseminated abroad and made widely known.

Some will try to insist that Congress must pass legislation at the end of the attainder trial, formally imposing punishment on the accused, otherwise there is no bill of attainder. That opinion is mistaken. "As originally introduced and employed in England," the form could be either "the parliamentary enactment or declaration of attainder."[214] A declaration is sufficient.

The historical reasons for having legislative bills is worth noting. Centuries ago there was only one form of mass media, namely, the printing press. In republics, where representatives of the people discourse with one another and then enact legislation, there is a time-honored requirement that the legislature must make its drafts of proposed laws available to the public so that the people can consider the matter and advise their representatives how to vote.

The drafts are printed as bills. Those bills are then "published," meaning that they are widely distributed and proclaimed to the electorate.

In the early days of "bills of attainder," the allegations were printed in a bill which was then distributed throughout the realm to be read aloud by couriers in the marketplace or to be read by individuals at the county seat or town hall.

When the bill was distributed from town to town and the allegations in the bill became generally known, the public would be induced by the official nature of the act to agree with the legislature's low opinion of the accused, or at least to have sincere doubts. The spreading abroad of these pronouncements of guilt was what "attainted" the accused. His name became a household word, and everywhere there would be some who believed him to be guilty of the odious crimes pronounced by the legislature.

The purpose for writing the bill was to record the statements alleging guilt, and the purpose of publishing the bill was to place those accusations before the attention of the public.

The Information Superhighway

Electronic communication now accomplishes in split seconds what used to take days, weeks, or months by the distribution of printed bills. Congress can now get its message to the public by satellite television, and by radio and TV simulcasts. In 1987, modern technology made it possible for Congress to publish its accusations of guilt moment by moment as it conducted the legislative trial.

The technological revolution puts a whole new spin on the Constitution's prohibition against "bills" of attainder. If the guilt is alleged and recorded (in this case digitally encoded), and then published in such a way as to make it generally known to the public (as for example by "wall to wall" television coverage), the attainting process forbidden in the Constitution has in fact taken place.

Since what is at stake is a constitutional principle, we need not agree with those who insist that a bill of attainder only takes place the old fashioned way – by Congress passing a bill at the end of a political trial, legislating the death, exile, or forfeiture of the houses and lands of the accused, and then publishing the bill by having it carried on horseback to the towns of the realm.

Otherwise, Congress can ruin people with political trials, and wreak incredible harm upon them with impunity, so long as Congress does not make the mistake of enacting legislation at the end of the hearing, imposing a criminal penalty on a named party. Such a wooden view of bills of attainder can only be true if our rights and liberties are secured by a wooden Constitution.

The Larger Principle

It is not enough to say that our Founding Fathers wished only to outlaw bills of attainder as they were known and practiced in England. The prohibition in the state and federal constitutions is meant to remedy the underlying political distemper that causes legislatures to act in such a fashion in the first place.

The courts of New York in 1894 gave this explanation for the constitutional prohibitions of bills of attainder:

> The possible tyranny by a majority of a representative assemblage was well understood and appreciated, and there were for that reason many provisions inserted in the Constitution limiting the exercise of legislative power by Federal and also by state legislatures.[215]

An opinion by a Kentucky judge in 1863 said the reasons included

> to get rid of the gross injustice, oppressions, and tyranny of the . . . machinery of the English government, often invoked to crush and ruin those who had become obnoxious to the reigning dynasty, . . .[216]

Justice Chase, in one of the first cases ever before the United States Supreme Court (Calder v Bull, 1798), made this insightful remark about bills of attainder:

> These acts were legislative judgments; and an exercise of judicial power. Sometimes they . . . declared acts to be treason which were not treason . . . at other times they violated the rules of evidence . . . received evidence without oath

> . . . or [required the testimony] of the wife against the husband; or other testimony which the courts of justice would not admit; at other times they inflicted punishments where the party was not, by law, liable to any punishment; . . . on the ground . . . that the safety of the kingdom depended on the . . . punishment of the offender. . . . With very few exceptions, the advocates . . . were stimulated by ambition, or personal resentment, and vindictive malice.[217]

Justice Chase must have turned over in his grave during the televised Iran/Contra political inquisition televised in the summer of 1987. Writing in the same 1798 case, Justice Iredell observed:

> Rival factions, in their efforts to crush each other, have superseded all the forms, and suppressed all the sentiments, of justice; while attainders, on the principle of retaliation and proscription, have marked all the vicissitudes of party triumph. The temptation to such abuses of power is unfortunately too alluring for human virtue; and, therefore the framers of the American Constitutions have wisely denied to the respective legislatures, Federal as well as state, the possession of the power itself.[218]

Can anyone doubt that the effect, if not the purpose, of the televised hearings in the summer of 1987 was to stigmatize Oliver North and to destroy his reputation so that he would lose all respect in the community and possibly never again hold a government job or public office? Is there any doubt that he was subjected to official ridicule and declared by members of Congress to be odious, dangerous, disloyal and treasonous? The quotes by Congressmen are a matter of public record.

Certainly the lectures, harangues, and public chastisement of North before a television audience is no less a declaration than if Congress had written it in a bill.

An attainder occurs when the effect of an action of Congress is to inflict punishment without the safeguards of a judicial trial and is determined by no previous law or fixed rule. Congress's actions punished North by seeking to make it impossible for him to serve in the government and by depriving him of his civil rights.

He was denied an impartial trial before an impartial jury. At his political hearing he was not permitted full legal representation by his attorney (remember Attorney Sullivan's famous outburst "I'm not a potted plant!"). He was denied the right to be confronted by the witnesses against him. He was compelled to incriminate himself on twisted readings and misapplications of public laws. He was subjected to humiliation and denial of due process.

He was accused of common law sedition and treason against the Constitution. He was repeatedly accused of illegal, unethical, and disreputable acts, including violating his military oath, which is punishable under the Uniform Code of Military Justice.

The committee made various conclusory assertions of criminal guilt, some open, some by innuendo, tantamount to a legislative judgment of conviction.

The machinery of the Committee was oppressive, invoked to crush and ruin those who had become obnoxious to the reigning dynasty in Congress.

The Committee departed from ordinary Congressional rules, restricted the assistance of defense lawyers, and members on occasion affirmed that the accused was unfit to continue serving the government.

Through the Committee, Congress indulged in a thinly veiled exercise of judicial power, violating the rules of evidence, proposing to establish the violation of some federal law, and intruding on the husband-wife relationship of the Norths (defense counsel had to beg that Mrs. North not be called as a witness).

The Committee was not impartial, but disguised the punishment of North so that it would not be apparently violative of law. As a pretext, Congress used the argument that the safety of the Constitution and of the government required these abuses. The end result was to attempt to disqualify Colonel North from holding a position of trust. In short, the Congress's treatment of Colonel North qualifies as a bill of attainder in violation of Article 1, Clause 9, Section 3 of the U.S. Constitution.

ENDNOTES

[1]"No Bill of Attainder or ex post facto Law shall be passed." [U.S. Constitution, Article 1, Section 9, Clause 3.]

"Attaint: To condemn by a sentence of attainder. To impart stigma to; to disgrace. To accuse or prove guilty."

"Attainder: The loss of . . . civil rights. Dishonor."

"Bill of Attainder: A . . . legislative act pronouncing a person guilty of a crime, usually treason, without trial. . . ." [American Heritage Dictionary.]

[2] "Legislative acts, no matter what their form, that apply either to named individuals or to easily ascertainable members of a group in such a way as to inflict punishment on them without judicial trial are bills of attainder prohibited by the Constitution." U.S. v Lovett, 328 U.S. 303, 315, 90 L.Ed. 1252.

"When our Constitution and Bill of Rights were written, our ancestors had ample reason to know that legislative trials and punishments were too dangerous to liberty to exist in the nation of free men they envisioned. And so they proscribed bills of attainder." Ibid., 318.

[3]My criticisms of Congress must be understood in the following light. Not all Democrats were against Oliver North and not all Republicans were for him. Some democrats supported Reagan's policies, some Republicans did not. And not every Representative or Senator agreed with conducting the public hearings. A strong and vocal minority disagreed with the Iran/Contra televised spectacle. This complex mixture presents an immediate challenge to precise definition of terms. However, since Congress is a majoritarian body, the acts of the majority represent the whole. Therefore, I will use the term Congress to represent the acts of the whole, and of the majority of the select committees.

[4]Willian Cohen, Jonathan D. Varat, Constitutional Law: Cases and Materials (Westbury, N.Y.: Foundation Press, 1993), at 233-234. Emphasis added.

[5]Cohen & Varat, at 419.

[6]Quoted in, Cohen & Varat, at 418.

[7]"The President, Vice President, and all civil officers of the United States, shall be removed from office on impeachment for, and conviction of, treason, bribery, or other high crimes and misdemeanors." U.S. Constitution, Article 2, Section 4.

[8]"The House of Representatives . . . shall have the sole power of impeachment. U.S. Constitution, Article 1, Section 2, Clause 5.

[9]"The Senate shall have the sole power to try all impeachments. When sitting for that purpose, they shall be on oath or affirmation. When the President of the United States is tried, the Chief Justice shall preside; and no person shall be convicted without the concurrence of two thirds of the members present." U.S. Constitution, Article 1, Section 3, Clause 6.
"Judgment in cases of impeachment shall not extend further than to removal from office, and disqualification to hold and enjoy any office of honour, trust or profit, under the United States; but the party convicted shall nevertheless be liable and subject to indictment, trial, judgment, and punishment according to law." U.S. Constitution, Article 1, Section 3, Clause 7.

[10]"The trial of all crimes, except in cases of impeachment, shall be by jury; and such trial shall be held in the State where the said crimes shall have been committed; but when not committed within any state, the trial shall be at such place or places as the Congress may by law have directed." U.S. Constitution, Article 3, Section 2, Clause 3.

[11]"During fiscal year 1985, no funds available to the Central Intelligence Agency, the Department of Defense, or any other agency or entity of the United States involved in intelligence activities may be obligated or expended for the purpose or which would have the effect of supporting, directly or indirectly, military or paramilitary operations in Nicaragua by any nation, group, organization, movement, or individual."

[12]The Boland Amendments pertained to funds appropriated through the Intelligence Authorization Act and the Continuing Appropriations Act. The Intelligence Appropriations Act regulated the manner in which money would be disbursed for use by the intelligence community. The various agencies and organizations which were part of that community were identified and listed by Congress. The NSC was not on the list, nor was it a recipient of any of the related funds.

[13]Quoted in, Nowak & Rotunda, at 199.

[14]Cited by Douglas Jeffrey in Claremont Review of Books, Spring 1987, p. 9.

[15]See, Richard L. Perry, Sources of our Liberties: Documentary Origins of Individual liberties in the United States Constitution and Bill of Rights, Rev. ed. (Chicago: American Bar Foundation, 1978), 125 - 142.

[16]Perry, Sources of Our Liberties, 133.

[17]Perry, Sources of Our Liberties, 132.

[18]This is not intended in any way to denigrate the heroic and selfless role played by Admiral John Poindexter. His tribulations and unjust suffering should not be slighted. However, because Admiral Poindexter was North's superior, he had to "fall on his own sword" to protect the President. Once having done so, he was no longer in any position to carry on the fight.

[19]Lawrence E. Walsh, Final Report of the Independent Counsel for Iran/Contra Matters, Volume 1: Investigations and Prosecutions (August 4, 1993; Washington, D.C.), p. 561, Concluding Observations. [Emphasis added.]

[20]Ibid.

[21]Ibid.

[22]Ibid., 562.

[23]Ibid.

[24]Ibid., 565. [Emphasis added.]

[25]Ibid., 58.

[26]Ibid., 63.

[27]Ibid., 66.

[28]James Madison, in Federalist Paper 48 warned of this ploy used by legislatures to seize power: "It is evident that none [of the three branches of government] ought to possess, directly or indirectly, an overruling influence over the other in the administration of their respective powers. . . . If, therefore, the legislature assumes executive and judiciary powers, no opposition is likely to be made; nor, if made, can be effectual; because in that case they may put their proceedings into the form of acts of Assembly, which will render them obligatory on the other branches. They have accordingly, in many instances, decided rights which should have been left to judiciary controversy, and the direction of the executive, during the whole time of their session, is becoming habitual and familiar." In, Clinton Rossiter, ed., The Federalist Papers: Alexander Hamilton, James Madison, John Jay (New York: New American Library, 1961), at 309 and 311 .

"We have seen that the tendency of republican governments is to an aggrandizement of the legislative at the expense of the other departments. . . . But the legislative party would not only be able to plead their cause most successfully with the people. They would probably be constituted themselves the judges." Ibid., Federalist Paper 50, at 316-317.

[29]See Appendix A for a copy of the January 17, 1986 presidential finding written by Oliver North.

[30]See, Charles J. Cooper, Assistant Attorney General, Memorandum for the Attorney General Re: Legal Authority for Recent Covert Arms Transfers to Iran (December 17, 1986), reprinted in Iran-Contra Congressional Hearings, 100-6, at 630.

[31]See, page 742 et seq., Comments in Response to the Final Report of Independent Counsel Lawrence E. Walsh, December 3, 1993, in Volume 3, Final Report of the Independent Counsel for Iran/Contra Matters (December 3, 1993, Washington, D.C.).

[32]Edwin Meese III, Comments in Response to the Final Report of Independent Counsel Lawrence E. Walsh, December 3, 1993, in Volume 3, Final Report of the Independent Counsel for Iran/Contra Matters (December 3, 1993, Washington, D.C.), 419.

[33]Proverbs 22:1 (King James Version). The New International Version translates this verse as: "A good name is more desirable than great riches; to be esteemed is better than silver or gold."

[34]Numbers 13:16-17; and, Numbers 21:32.

[35]Numbers 21:32-35.

[36]Numbers 13:17 - 14:9.

[37]Joshua 2:3.

[38]Hebrews 11:31 and James 2:25 (New Testament).

[39]Exodus 1:15

[40]Exodus 1:18.

[41]Exodus 1:20-21.

[42]See note 3 above.

[43]An apparent freedom of choice with no real alternative. (After Thomas Hobson, the English liveryman, who required his customers to take the next available horse rather than give them a choice.) Source, American Heritage Dictionary.

[44]See discussion of U.S. v Lovett in Appendix B.

[45]Walsh, Final Report, Volume 3, at 406.

[46]"Where immunized testimony is used before a grand jury, the prohibited act is simultaneous and coterminous with the presentation; indeed, they are one and the same. . . . [T]he grand jury process itself is violated and corrupted, and the indictment becomes indistinguishable from the constitutional and statutory transgression. . . . [U]se [of compelled testimony] is a wrong that goes to the quick of the indictment. This distinction eludes the IC and the District Court; . . ." 910 F.2d 843, 869 (D.C.Cir. 1990). Emphasis added.

"Where the prosecution reneges on this constitutionally-mandated bargain and presents the immunized testimony to the grand jury, the constitutional violation is part and parcel of the grand jury process." 920 F.2d 940, 948 (D.C.Cir. 1990).

[47]Walsh, Final Report, Volume 1, 26.

[48]Ibid, at 27.

[49]Ibid.

[50]Ibid., at 28.

[51]Ibid., at 33.

[52]Ibid., at 108.

[53]Ibid., at 117.

[54]U.S. v North, 708 F.Supp. 399, 401 (D.D.C. 1988).

[55]U.S. v. Poindexter, 698 F.Supp. 300, 319 (D.D.C. 1988) June 22, 1988. The case is so named because at this point in the trial, the prosecutions of Poindexter, North, and Hakim had not be severed.

[56]U.S. v North, 708 F.Supp. 389 (D.D.C. 1988).

[57]Walsh, Final Report, Volume 1, at 28.

[58]Ibid., Volume 1, note 40, at 44.

[59]Ibid., Volume 3, at 604.

[60]Ibid., Volume 1, at xvii.

[61]Ibid., Volume 1, at xv: "Independent Counsel has concluded that the President's most senior advisers and the Cabinet members on the National Security Council participated in the strategy to make National Security staff members McFarlane, Poindexter and North the scapegoats whose sacrifice would protect the Reagan Administration in its final two years."

[62]U.S. v North, 910 F.2d 843 (D.C. Cir 1990), Decided July 20, 1990, as amended Aug. 22, 1990, at page 932 (Concurring opinion).

[63]Ibid., 910 F.2d 843, at 933, 934, and footnote 2.

[64]Ibid.

[65]U.S. v North, 910 F.2d 843, 863 (D.C.Cir. 1990), and U.S. v North, 920 F.2d 940, 947 (D.C.Cir. 1990).

[66]Ibid., 910 F.2d 843, 851.

[67]Ibid., at 863.

[68]Ibid., at 878.

[69]Ibid., at 885. Italics in original. Emphasis added.

[70]Ibid., at 886.

[71]Ibid., at 887. Italics in original. Emphasis added.

[72]Ibid., at 887.

[73]Ibid., at 888. Italics in original. Emphasis added.

[74]Ibid., at 888.

[75]Ibid., at 945. Italics in original. Emphasis added.

[76]Ibid., at 910.

[77]Using the wrong form is reversible error. The Federal Rules of Criminal Procedure require the indictment to have a separate Count for each offense. Courts in the 8th circuit have reversed convictions for the "two shots for one count" verdict form. The First Circuit calls the practice error. See, 910 F.2d 843, 911.

[78]Ibid., at 945.

[79]See, Joseph E. Blackburn, Jr., "North was A Soldier Serving His Superiors — and Abandoned," Richmond Times-Dispatch, Wednesday, June 1, 1994, at A 11.

[80]Walsh, Final Report, Volume 2, at 217. Emphasis added.

[81]U.S. v North, 910 F.2d 843, 881 (D.D.Cir. 1990). Emphasis added.

[82]See, Federalist Papers 48 - 51. "But the great security against a gradual concentration of the several powers in the same department consists in giving to those who administer each department the necessary constitutional means and personal motives to resist encroachments from the other. The provision for defense must in this, as in all other cases, be made commensurate to the danger of attack. Ambition must be made to counteract ambition. The interest of the man must be connected with the constitutional rights of the place. It may be a reflection on human nature that such devices should be necessary to control the abuses of government." James Madison, Federalist Paper 51. In, Clinton Rossiter, ed., The

Federalist Papers: Alexander Hamilton, James Madison, John Jay (New York: New American Library, 1961), at 322.

[83]Ibid., compare note 26 above, and Federalist 73 at pages 442 et seq.

[84]See, Nowak & Rotunda, Constitutional Law, at 239-255.

[85]Federalist Paper 50 warns of the danger of two branches combining against the third in support of a wrong principle. See, Clinton Rossiter, ed., The Federalist Papers: Alexander Hamilton, James Madison, John Jay (New York: New American Library, 1961), at 314.

[86]U.S. v North, 910 F.2d 843, 883 (D.D.Cir. 1990). Emphasis added.

[87]Ibid., at 883.

[88]Ibid., at 883-884.

[89]Ibid.

[90]Ibid., at 884.

[91]Ibid., Silberman dissent, at 947.

[92]Walsh, Final Report, Volume 2, at 2-3.

[93]To provide himself with an excuse to drop the conspiracy charge and save face, Walsh subpoenaed records which he knew that Attorney General Thornburgh would not declassify. When Thornburgh refused to turn them over, Walsh dropped the first four Counts on the pretext that the government was blocking him from proving his case. The documents he sought were unnecessry to his claim. The conspiracy charge rested not on the classified documents, but on whether Walsh's conspiracy theory was valid under the law. It was not. See, Walsh, Final Report, Volume 1, at 55.

[94]Ibid., Volume 2, at 200.

[95]Congress claimed to have a right to know. Therefore even if the President's actions were legal, and even if he believed Congress did not have a right to know, at least not yet, to deceive Congress by not giving them the truth would be a crime. In short, it is a crime to keep secret your legal activities.

[96]Perjury is supposed to be a crime of intent, that is, you can only be guilty of perjury if you intentionally make a false statement which is then contradicted by another sworn statement. However, motive is something that can be implied, therefore, innocent differences in one's testimony can be made to look like perjury.

[97]U.S. v North, 708 F.Supp. 364, 366 (D.D.C. 1988).

[98]Ibid., at 383.

[99]Ibid., at 383. Emphasis added.

[100]He specifically objected to a number of summaries as being inaccurate. Nevertheless, he was not allowed access to the originals nor to submit them as evidence at trial.

[101]U.S. v North, 910 F.2d 843, 935 (D.C.Cir. 1990).

[102]Ibid., at 936.

[103]Ibid., (Judge Silberman's explanation of Wardius).

[104]This is not to say that he did not make false statements. This simply means that the whole rigmarole about him being a convicted felon for lying to Congress is a complete myth. His actions were found by the jury not to be in violation of any law. And for purposes of Iran/Contra that is the entire point.

[105]Joseph E. Blackburn, Jr., "North was A Soldier Serving His Superiors — and Abandoned," Richmond Times-Dispatch, Wednesday, June 1, 1994, at A 11.

[106]U.S. v North, 910 F.2d 843, 856-858 (D.C.Cir. 1990).

[107]All these possibilities are noted by the Court, Ibid., at pages 857-858.

[108]Ibid., at 856.

[109]Ibid., at 924.

[110]U.S. v North, 910 F.2d 843, 915 (D.C.Cir. 1990), dissenting opinion.

[111]Ibid., at 916.

[112]Ibid., at 918.

[113]Ibid.

[114]U.S. v North, 920 F.2d 940, 944 (D.C. Cir. 1990), Nov 30, 1990.

[115]U.S. v North, 910 F.2d 843, 861. Emphasis added.

[116]116 U.S. 616, 631-32, 6 S.Ct. 524, 533, 29 L.Ed. 746 (1886). Emphasis added.

[117]U.S. v North, 910 F.2d 843,853. Emphasis added.

[118]Federal Use Immunity Statute 18 U.S.C. § 6002:

> Whenever a witness refuses, on the basis of his privilege against self-incrimination, to testify or provide other information in a proceeding before or ancillary to –
> (1) a court or grand jury of the United States,
> (2) an agency of the United States, or
> (3) either House of Congress, a joint committee of the two Houses, or a committee or a subcommittee of either House,
> and the person presiding over the proceeding communicates to the witness an order issued under this part, the witness may not refuse to comply with the order on the basis of his privilege against self-incrimination; but no testimony or other information compelled under the order (or any information directly or indirectly derived from such

testimony or information) may be used against the witness in any criminal case, except a prosecution for perjury, giving a false statement, or otherwise failing to comply with the order.

[119]Kastigar v. United States, 406 U.S. 441, 92 S.Ct. 1653, 32 L.Ed.2d 212 (1972).

[120]See, "What Constitutes Bill of Attainder Under the Federal Constitution," Annotation, 90 L.Ed. 1267-1292.

[121]U.S. v North, 910 F.2d 843, at 861, citing United States v Apfelbaum, 445 U.S. 115 (1980).

[122]Ibid.

[123]Ibid., at 861. See for example, Monroe v. United States, 234 F.2d 49 (D.C. Cir).

[124]Haynes Johnson, Tracy Thompson, "North Charges Dismissed at Request of Prosecutor: Special Counsel Drops Charges Against North in Iran-Contra Affair," The Washington Post, Tuesday, September 17, 1991, A1 and A16.

[125]U.S. v North, 910 F.2d 843, 861. Emphasis added.

[126]Ibid., at 865.

[127]Ibid. Emphasis added.

[128]Ibid., at 856.

[129]Ibid., at 860.

[130]Ibid., at 863.

[131]Ibid., at 864.

[132]Ibid., at 860. Emphasis added.

[133]Ibid., at 869.

[134]Ibid., at 869.

[135]Ibid., at 869.

[136]Ibid., at 863.

[137]Ibid., at 856.

[138]Ibid., at 871.

[139]Ibid., at 863.

[140]Ibid., at 862.

[141]Ibid., at 860.

[142]Ibid., at 862.

[143]Ibid., at 865.

[144]Ibid., at 867.

[145]Ibid., at 867.

[146]Ibid., at 869.

[147]Ibid., at 869.

[148]U.S. v North, 920 F.2d 940, 947.

[149]Ibid., at 944.

[150]Walsh, Final Report, Volume 3, at page 2.

[151]Ibid., Abrams gives example.

[152]Final Report, Volume 3, at 7. Armitage gives three pages of examples as "graphic evidence of the Independent Counsel's misstatements. . . ."

[153]Ibid., at 9.

[154]Ibid., at 11.

[155]Final Report, Volume 3, at 21.

[156]Ibid., at 30.

[157]See page 32, Ibid.

[158]Final Report, Volume 3, at 50.

[159]Final Report, Volume 3, at 53.

[160]See, Final Report, Volume 3, at 65.

[161]Corr presents 27 pages of documentary proof.

[162] Final Report, Volume 3, at 95.

[163]At 95.

[164]At 95.

[165]Final Report, Volume 3, at 98.

[166]Ibid., at 98.

[167]Ibid., at 223.

[168]See, Final Report, Volume 3, 271 et seq.

[169]Final Report, Volume 3, at 310.

[170]Ibid., at 324.

[171]Ibid., at 324.

[172]Ibid., at 324.

[173]Ibid., at 325.

[174]Ibid., at 325.

[175]Ibid., at 326.

[176]Final Report, Volume 3, at 406.

[177]Ibid., at 406-407.

[178]Ibid., at 407.

[179]Ibid., at 407.

[180]Ibid., at 408.

[181]Ibid., at 419 et seq.

[182]Ibid., at 407.

[183]Ibid., at 430.

[184]Ibid., at 432.

[185]Ibid., at 432.

[186]Ibid., at 432-433.

[187]Ibid., at 433.

[188]Ibid., at 433.

[189]Ibid., at 434.

[190]Ibid., at 434-435.

[191]Ibid., at 436.

[192]Ibid., at 437.

[193]Ibid., at 437.

[194]Ibid., at 437.

[195]Final Report, Volume 3, at 643.

[196]Ibid., at 644.

[197]Ibid., at 645.

[198]Ibid., at 657.

[199]Ibid., at 659.

[200]Ibid., at 660.

[201]Ibid., at 664-668.

[202]Ibid., at 665-666.

[203]Ibid., at 666-672.

[204]Final Report, Volume 3, at 798.

[205]Ibid., at 798.

[206]Ibid., at 989-799.

[207]United States v Lovett, 328 U.S. 303, 90 L.ed. 1252 (June 3, 1946), at 1259.

[208]Ibid.

[209]Ibid., at 1260.

[210]Ibid.

[211]Ibid.

[212]Ibid.

[213]**§ 601.1 Jurisdiction of the Independent Counsel: Iran/Contra**

(a) The Independent Counsel Iran/Contra has jurisdiction to investigate to the maximum extent authorized by part 600 of this chapter whether any person or group of persons currently described in section 591 of title 28 of the U.S. Code, including Lieutenant Colonel Oliver L. North, other United States Government officials, or other individuals or organizations acting in concert with Lt. Col. North, or with other U.S. Government officials, has committed a violation of any federal criminal law, as referred to in section 591 of title 28 of the U.S. Code, . . .

(b) The Independent Counsel Iran/Contra shall have jurisdiction and authority to investigate other allegations or evidence of violation of any federal criminal law by Oliver L. North, and any person or entity heretofore referred to, . . .

52 Federal Rules 7272, March 10, 1987; 52 Federal Rules 9241, March 23, 1987, 28 CFR chap. 6,

[214]See, "What Constitutes Bill of Attainder Under the Federal Constitution," Annotation, 90 L.Ed. 1267, 1268.

[215]Ibid., at 1269.

[216]Ibid.

[217]Ibid., at 1270.

[218]Ibid.

Select Bibliography

Blackburn, Joseph E., Jr. "North was A Soldier Serving His Superiors — and Abandoned," Richmond Times-Dispatch, Wednesday, June 1, 1994, at A 11.

Code of Federal Regulations. 52 Federal Rules 7272, March 10, 1987; 52 Federal Rules 9241, March 23, 1987, 28 CFR chap. 6,

Cohen, Willian, and Jonathan D. Varat. Constitutional Law: Cases and Materials. Westbury, N.Y.: Foundation Press, 1993.

Federal Use Immunity Statute. 18 U.S.C. § 6002.

Johnson, Haynes, and Tracy Thompson. "North Charges Dismissed at Request of Prosecutor: Special Counsel Drops Charges Against North in Iran-Contra Affair," The Washington Post, Tuesday, September 17, 1991, A1 and A16.

Kastigar v. United States, 406 U.S. 441, 92 S.Ct. 1653, 32 L.Ed.2d 212 (1972).

Monroe v. United States, 234 F.2d 49 (D.C. Cir).

North v. Walsh, 881 F.2d 1088 (D.C. Cir) 1989.

Nowak, John E., and Ronald D. Rotunda. Constitutional Law. 4th ed. St. Paul, Minn: West Publishing, 1991.

Perry, Richard L. Sources of our Liberties: Documentary Origins of Individual liberties in the United States Constitution and Bill of Rights. Rev. ed. Chicago: American Bar Foundation, 1978.

Rossiter, Clinton, ed. The Federalist Papers: Alexander Hamilton, James Madison, John Jay. New York: New American Library, 1961.

U.S. v. Lovett, 328 U.S. 303, 90 L.ed. 1252 (June 3, 1946).

U.S. v. North, 698 F.Supp. 300 (D.D.C. 1988), June 16, 1988.

U.S. v. North, 698 F.Supp. 322 (D.D.C. 1988), July 8, 1988.

U.S. v. North, 708 F.Supp. 364 (D.D.C. 1988), Nov. 10, 1988.

U.S. v. North, 708 F.Supp. 370 (D.D.C. 1988), Nov. 17, 1988.

U.S. v. North, 708 F.Supp. 372 (D.D.C. 1988), Nov. 29, 1988.

U.S. v. North, 708 F.Supp. 375 (D.D.C. 1988), Nov. 29, 1988.

U.S. v. North, 708 F.Supp. 380 (D.D.C. 1988), Nov. 29, 1988.

U.S. v. North, 708 F.Supp. 385 (D.D.C. 1988), Dec. 2, 1988.

U.S. v. North, 708 F.Supp. 387 (D.D.C. 1988), Dec. 2, 1988.

U.S. v. North, 708 F.Supp. 389 (D.D.C. 1988), Dec. 12, 1988.

U.S. v. North, 708 F.Supp. 399 (D.D.C. 1988), Dec. 23, 1988.

U.S. v. North, 708 F.Supp. 402 (D.D.C. 1989), Jan. 27, 1989.

U.S. v. North, 713 F.Supp. 1436 (D.D.C. 1989), Jan. 19, 1989.

U.S. v. North, 713 F.Supp. 1441 (D.D.C. 1989), Feb. 9, 1989.

U.S. v. North, 713 F.Supp. 1442 (D.D.C. 1989), Feb. 17, 1989.

U.S. v. North, 713 F.Supp. 1444 (D.D.C. 1989), Feb. 23, 1989.

U.S. v. North, 713 F.Supp. 1445 (D.D.C. 1989), March 16, 1989.

U.S. v. North, 713 F.Supp. 1446 (D.D.C. 1989), March 17, 1989.

U.S. v. North, 713 F.Supp. 1447 (D.D.C. 1989), March 21, 1989.

U.S. v. North, 713 F.Supp. 1448 (D.D.C. 1989), March 31, 1989.

U.S. v. North, 713 F.Supp. 1450 (D.D.C. 1989), April 5, 1989.

U.S. v. North, 713 F.Supp. 1452 (D.D.C. 1989), April 18, 1989.

U.S. v. North, 713 F.Supp. 1453 (D.D.C. 1989), April 19, 1989.

U.S. v. North, 910 F.2d 843 (D.C. Cir 1990). Decided July 20, 1990, as amended Aug. 22, 1990.

U.S. v. North, 920 F.2d 940 (D.C. Cir. 1990), Nov. 30, 1990

U.S. v. Poindexter, 698 F.Supp. 316 (D.D.C. 1988), June 22, 1988.

Walsh, Lawrence E. Final Report of the Independent Counsel for Iran/Contra Matters. 3 vols. Volume 1: Investigations and Prosecutions. Volume 2: Indictments, Plea Agreements, Interim Reports to the Congress, and Administrative Matters. Volume 3: Comments and Materials Submitted by Individuals and Their Attorneys Responding to Volume 1 of the Final Report. Washington, D.C.: August 4, 1993.

"What Constitutes Bill of Attainder Under the Federal Constitution," Annotation, 90 L.Ed. 1267-1292.